exploring ireland's middle kingdom

a guide to the ancient kingdom of meath

exploring ireland's middle kingdom

a guide to
the ancient kingdom of meath

VALERIE PAKENHAM

SOMERVILLE PRESS

Somerville Press Ltd,
Dromore, Bantry, Co. Cork, Ireland

Text © Valerie Pakenham 2021
Drawings by Hector McDonnell © Hector McDonnell 2021

Designed by Jane Stark
Typeset in Adobe Garamond Pro
seamistgraphics@gmail.com

ISBN: 978-1-8382544-1-4

Printed and bound in Spain
by GraphyCems, Villatuerta, Navarra

For Thomas, Hanne, Christopher and Robert
who have helped me explore
the Middle Kingdom.

Ruins of Clonmacnoise. GEORGE PETRIE, FROM J.N. BREWER'S *BEAUTIES OF IRELAND*, 1825

contents

preface

I began writing this book during lockdown in the spring of 2020, not the best moment perhaps to begin a guidebook. But this has been a long planned for project and lockdowns have created the perfect opportunity for writing. I have spent much of my life exploring the ancient kingdom of Meath or Middle Kingdom, and have always wished to encourage others to do the same.

Meath's ancient boundaries have fluctuated over the centuries, but for over 3,000 years from the Iron Age to the 16th century, it incorporated roughly what are now Meath, Westmeath and most of Louth and Longford, and so I have cast my net over these four counties with one or two exceptions. To make places easy to find, I have divided them into eight sections around the principal towns with maps attached. The places listed largely follow my own tastes and interests, and many can be explored free of charge.

Eastern Meath and Louth have always been the richer and better known parts of the old Middle Kingdom – the Boyne valley and its castles and great Neolithic monuments have attracted visitors for at least two hundred and fifty years. Western Meath and Longford are less well known. But their wide landscapes of lakes and hills and bogs form to me the perfect complement to the rich more densely populated plains further east and hold just as much fascinating early history. Until the reconquest of Ireland in Tudor times, this was still Gaelic country, well outside the Norman Pale and Norman outposts were under constant attack. Only a few miles from where I live is one example, – the beautiful abbey of Fore, sacked repeatedly throughout the middle ages by "Irish rebels" until its final dissolution by Henry VIII.

Most of the illustration for this book I owe to Hector McDonnell. Hector is not only a wonderful artist, but an archaeologist who has written several books on Ireland's early history himself. For colour, I have relied mainly on the 18th and early 19th century prints and watercolours made when "ancient Ireland" was being discovered and the rage for Irish antiquities was at its height. Many of these provide valuable historical records in themselves – as do George Petrie's beautifully detailed pen and ink drawings made a generation later. My thanks to the librarians of the Royal Irish Academy, the Irish Architectural Archive and the National Library of Ireland who so kindly provided these to me during lockdown and to Charlotte Bonar Law who supplied more from her father's private collection. The charming colour print of Newbridge House was sent me by Alec Cobbe, the picture of Wellington on his pillar in Trim was lent to me by Joseph Carr and Mary Smyth lent me her drawing of Granard. Robert O'Byrne and my husband, Thomas Pakenham have generously provided colour photographs of other places listed.

Many other friends have helped with this book – Christopher and Hanne Grey have arranged many hugely enjoyable tours of Meath. Noel French explained to us in situ the wonders of Newtown Trim. Aisling Law showed us the wonderful view of the Boyne and the great Neolithic mounds of Brú na Bóinne from her garden at Rosnaree (said to be where the High King, Cormac mac Art had his final dwelling place). Emily Naper lent me many books on the mysteries of Neolithic art at Loughcrew and elsewhere. Ruth Illingworth and Bartle Darcy gave me much additional information on the history of Westmeath and Longford and read early drafts of the book. Aidan Walshe also kindly read my introductory history and corrected Irish spellings. John Corrigan painstakingly created the detailed maps I needed. Octavia Tulloch spent many hours "transferring" pictures for me, and wrestling with technical blips. Finally my thanks to my publishers, Jane and Andrew Russell, for their encouragement and support and to Jane Stark the book's designer for her skill and patience.

For further reading, I would like to recommend the following: first, Sir William Wilde's *The Beauties of the Boyne and Its Tributary the Blackwater* first published in 1849 and republished in 2008. Sir William (father of Oscar) was an early collector of Irish folklore and his book is a treasure trove of local stories. *North Leinster* (1999) by Alistair Rowan and Christine Casey is a superb record of buildings of architectural or historical interest, in four counties and has an excellent essay to Meath's prehistory by George Eoghan.

Hector McDonnell's *Ireland's Other History* (2010) widens the canvas as an illustrated history of Ireland from Neolilithic times to the Normans, tracing successive waves of invaders and their cultures. Peter Harbison's book *Treasures of the Boyne Valley* (2003) has magnificent pictures and an enthralling text. Noel French's *Discovering the Boyne Valley* (2018) is a highly readable and more portable guide to the same area. Areas further west are covered in *Heritage Landscapes of the Irish Midlands* by P.J. Gibson (2007) with excellent maps. Ruth Illingworth's *Little Book of Westmeath* (2016) is a perfect pocket history of my own county. Thomas Dean's gazetteer of *The Gate Lodges of Leinster* will add interest to any journey – often marking the ghostly remains of a once great house or castle and its demesne.

Several websites have also been invaluable for background history; Robert O'Byrne's blog, *The Irish Aesthete* is an ongoing source of wonderful photographs and information on Ireland's heritage buildings of all kinds; *Megalithic Ireland* and *Ireland in Ruins* also explore many lesser known heritage sites in detail and give excellent first hand instructions on where and how to find them. Finally my thanks to the unknown multiple authors of Wikipedia – there is almost no place, person or historical event that I have failed to find on their amazing website.

piccure credics

Most of the illustrations in this book have been especially drawn for it by Hector McDonnell and are credited in his name. Other artists and sources are listed alphabetically below.

Gabriel Beranger, courtesy of the Royal Irish Academy, Dublin, p. 46, 49, 59, 61, 75.

Louisa Beaufort, courtesy of the Weston Library, Oxford, p. 37.

Adam Buck, courtesy of the National Gallery of Ireland, Dublin, p. 136.

Joseph Carr, private collection, p. 75.

Drogheda North of the River (anon.), courtesy of the National Library of Ireland, Dublin, p. 30/31.

William Frazer, courtesy of the National Library of Ireland, Dublin, p. 90.

Frances Edgeworth, courtesy of the Edgeworth Centre, Edgeworthstown, p. 24.

Daniel Grose, courtesy of Lord Rossmore, the Irish Architectural Archive, Dublin, p. 119, 121, 122, 124, 140, 141.

Francis Grose, courtesy of the Neptune Gallery, Dublin, p. 20, 33, 77; courtesy of the National Library of Ireland, Dublin, p. 45.

James Howley, *Follies and Garden Buildings of Ireland*, 1993, p. 91.

James Malton, private collection, p. 13.

John Nankivell, courtesy of the Irish Georgian Society, p. 26.

J.P. Neale, *View of Seats*, 1823, p. 55, 126.

Newbridge House, (anon.), courtesy of Alec Cobbe, p. 57.

Robert O'Byrne, p. 31, 40, 68, 86, 93.

Thomas Pakenham, p. 25, 95, 99, 100, 107, 109, 117, 139, 142.

George Petrie, Frontispiece from J.N. Brewer's *Beauties of Ireland*, 1825; T.K. Cromwell's *Excursions through Ireland*, 1821, p. 29, 35, 62, 77, 79, 80, 89, 102, 108. Reprinted in George Petrie, *The Re-discovery of Ireland's Past*, 2004, by Peter Murray, courtesy of the Crawford Gallery, Cork.

Mary Powys, private collection, p. 136.

Thomas Roberts, private collection, courtesy of the Pym Gallery, London, p. 65.

Mary Smyth, private collection, p. 133.

Westmeath Tourism, p. 14.

Wikimedia, p. 65, 131.

Map of Ireland circa 900 AD, showing the boundaries of the Middle Kingdom.
INSET: *Norman emblem for the Royal Kingdom of Meath.* SOURCE: WIKIMEDIA

a brief history of
the middle kingdom

The Middle Kingdom has always been hugely important in Irish myths and history. It once formed the fifth province of Ireland. According to legend, Ireland was originally divided by five brothers who met on the **Hill of Uisneach** to share out the island between them. They allotted their youngest brother Slaine (or Slanius in Latin) the central or smallest share. Whereupon, in the words of Gerald of Wales, the Norman historian of Ireland, "Slanius settled himself therein and called it Meath or Midhe, meaning the middle kingdom." Slaine is said to have later expanded his kingdom and become the first High King. His burial place is marked on the **Hill of Slane**, which takes its name from him.

The Franciscan tower crowning the Hill of Slane. JAMES MALTON 1803

Irish legends usually have a core of truth. On the Hill of Uisneach (now in modern Westmeath) you still see the **Stone of the Divisions**, or **Catstone**, an enormous glacial boulder said to mark where this division took place. The Hill of Uisneach was once also venerated as the resting place of the great sun god Lugh and the earth goddess Eriu (or Erin) from whom Ireland takes its name. In pagan times, every year a great festival called Bealtaine took place here to mark the beginning of summer. People came from all over Ireland to celebrate the event; two enormous bonfires were lit and their cattle would be driven between them to ensure their well being. Torches from the Beltaine

The Stone of Divisions or Catstone on the Hill of Uisneach. WESTMEATH TOURIST OFFICE

fires would then be carried back to tribal assembly places all over Ireland where new fires were lit and then taken to every dwelling.

In the 1st century AD, a powerful king of the Middle Kingdom, Tuathal Techtmar (Toole the Lawful) is said to have "persuaded" the other provincial kings to give up further territory to him as tributary or "mensal" land for his High Kingship. The boundaries of Midhe now extended from the Shannon to the Irish sea, encompassing parts of present day Offaly, Kildare, Cavan. Louth and Longford, as well as Meath and Westmeath. Tuathal also imposed a huge annual fine known as the Boru tribute (15,000 cows, pigs and sheep a year) on nearby Leinster, blood money for his daughters who had both died of misery and shame while married to Leinster's king. Given this and its fertile lands, Midhe soon became the richest of the five provinces. Tuathal moved the chief assembly point for tribal gatherings from the Hill of Uisneach to the **Hill of Tara** in the plain of Breda. Tara became the centre for huge feasts at the annual druidic Spring festival and the selection and ceremonial rituals of successive High Kings. Not surprisingly, most were chosen from the kings of Meath. Another important assembly point was at Tailtu or **Teltown**, (east of

Kells) for the annual feast of Lughnasa, the summer harvest festival and for competitive feats of strength and horsemanship, a kind of Irish version of the Olympic games.

In the fourth century and fifth centuries AD, however much of the enlarged middle kingdom was invaded by the Uí Néill tribes from Connaught who assumed the titles of Kings of Uisneach and Tara. The southern Uí Néill as they were known alternated with their kindred from the north as High Kings for the next 500 years. One of their strongholds was at **Dún na Sciath** beside **Lough Ennell** guarding the road from Tara to the royal burial grounds of **Clonmacnoise** and they exacted tribute from as far east as Viking Dublin. The Meath kings formed the chief resistance to Viking raids from east and west and in the 9th century, Malachy I brought about the downfall of Turgesius, the most powerful of the Viking warlords. (He was lured to an island in **Lough Owel** on the promise of a marriage with King Malachy's daughter and then captured and drowned.) Only in the 11th and 12th centuries, did the Uí Néill power begin to crumble, under pressure from the other provincial kings. Feuds and rivalries were constant. The Annals of the Four Masters compiled from early manuscripts record many of the High Kings meeting a violent death.

In 1167, Rory O'Connor of Connaught, the current High King, deposed Dermot McMurrough, the King of Leinster, ostensibly for having abducted a rival king's wife, but as part of an ongoing feud. McMurrough fled to France to beg help from Henry II who was campaigning there. Henry granted him leave to ask the Norman barons on the Welsh marches for aid. A small band of Welsh and Normans, led by the Earl of Pembroke, also known as Strongbow, landed in Waterford, made their way north, and duly re-instated Dermot McMurrough as king. In return McMurrough made Strongbow his heir, and when McMurrough died shortly afterwards, Strongbow claimed Leinster as his fiefdom. In October 1171 Henry II hastened to Ireland himself to assert his authority as overlord and as a counterweight to Strongbow, allotted the rich lands of Meath, to his trusted deputy, Hugh de Lacy. The kingdom of Meath was to remain at the centre of power.

All this is to jump ahead in time. Meath has far more ancient monuments than those left by the kings at Tara and Uisneach or their Norman successors. The first hunter gatherers had arrived here around 7,000 BC . Their flint tools and axes have been found around most of the Westmeath lakes and along the banks of the Boyne and Inny rivers. Around 3,900 BC, new groups of Neolithic farmers appeared, probably making their way across the narrow straits from Scotland, or even from as far away as western France. They brought cattle and sheep and seeds with them. (Irish Neolithic man still had no horses as yet.) They settled largely on the uplands, where they could graze their herds and grow crops. Much of western Meath was still marshy land and bog. But even here there were hills and fertile eskers suitable for farming, and the new settlers built timber causeways across the bogs. They built stone cairns and passage graves on hilltops for communal burial. There is a string of their cairns along a ridge (just east of modern Oldcastle) known as **Slieve na Cullagh** or the Loughcrew hills, one of the largest Neolithic cemeteries ever found in Europe.

There seems to have been a major environmental disaster about 3,195 BC, probably caused by a massive volcanic eruption on Iceland, which darkened the skies for almost ten years and must have seemed to herald the dying of the sun. Crops would have failed and many Neolithic settlers must

Newgrange entrance with roofbox.
HECTOR MCDONNELL

have died of starvation. Soon after, it seems, the survivors began to build vast mounds at a bend on the Boyne, now known collectively as **Brú na Bóinne** (the feasting hall of the river goddess Bóinne). The labour and skills needed to create them must have been immense. The bulk of them is made up of layers of pebbles from the river bed, but there are also quantities of white quartz stone brought from the Wicklow hills (50km to the south) and basins hollowed out in granite boulders brought from the Mourne mountains

16

(50km to the north). Inside them are long passages lined with large slabs of stone leading to a central chamber. In the case of two, **Newgrange** and **Dowth**, the sun lights up the central chamber at dawn on the shortest day of the year; while passages at **Knowth** are orientated to catch the dawn at the autumn and spring solstices. It is thought their purpose was to venerate the sun in the hope that it would not die again. Many of the large stone slabs are incised with mysterious symbols, some of which clearly represent the sun.

Smaller portal tombs or dolmens were also built. (**Proleek** and **Aughnacliff** are two examples). Later, stone circles were erected all over the British Isles and were often added to earlier religious sites, which were still venerated though no longer used for rituals. In medieval times, these were believed to have been built by druids' magic. Ireland was famous for its druids; one Welsh historian, Geoffrey of Monmouth, even claimed that Stonehenge had been wafted by Merlin from the Hill of Uisneach to its present resting place. But in the later Stone Age, there seem to have been no great communal undertakings on the scale of Brú na Bóinne. Between 2,400 and 2,000 BC, the Irish population seems to have been decimated by repeated famines or outbreaks of disease. Most of their later burials were for individuals. Climb any large hill in Meath or Westmeath and you are likely to find a cluster of burial mounds or barrows on its top. Some of these have been excavated and their grave goods show contact with the wider world, jet from Yorkshire or amber from the Baltic. Trade had already spread across the whole Atlantic fringe.

Around 2,000 BC, waves of new settlers arrived from Britain and Europe bringing advanced metal working techniques. They were probably lured to Ireland by reports of copper which they later learned to blend with Cornish tin. This is the start of the Bronze Age. Bronze daggers and swords are found all over Ireland. They also mined lead from Antrim, and gold from the Wicklow hills for ornament. Many centuries later, in the Iron Age (around 300 AD) a style known as "La Tène" spread to Ireland from Europe, resulting in elaborately inlaid weapons and belts, clasps, necklaces and collars. You can see wonderful examples in the Treasure section of the National Museum in Dublin and more are still being found. In Lough Derravaragh, a whole horde of gold ornaments was recently dug out of the mud. There is a famous poem by Tom Moore lamenting King Malachy's "lost collar of gold"; Malachy's collar may still be awaiting some lucky fisherman in a Westmeath lake.

There were still few large settlements: most Bronze or Iron Age families lived in the raths or ringforts which still litter the Irish landscape. (In the 18th century, these were often planted with trees as a feature in gentlemen's parks.) Farmers would drive their stock at night into an embanked enclosure probably ringed by a ditch and a palisade of wooden stakes. Larger ringforts were sometimes built for tribal gatherings with multiple surrounding ditches. (**Rath Airthur** at Donaghpatrick or the **Hill of Ward** are two examples.) In western Meath, which was full of lakes, minor kings built crannogs or artificial islands to which they could retreat for safety. (**Cro-inish** in Lough Ennell is one example.) It is estimated there are at least 50 crannogs in the Westmeath lakes alone.

Around the 5th century, the history of Meath was transformed by the coming of St Patrick. We know only a little about him although he did leave two authentic documents behind him describing important aspects of his life. Born into a well off Romano British family, he was captured by Irish raiders aged 16 and worked as a slave for seven years, herding cattle probably in Northern Ireland, before he managed to escape and find a boat back to Britain. He became a priest and then decided his mission was to bring Christianity to the poor and needy of Ireland. The Life of St Patrick written 200 years after his death relates that on Easter day, 432 AD, he lit a fire on the Hill of Slane as a deliberate challenge to the High King Loaghaire, who was about to celebrate the Spring solstice with a great fire on the Hill of Tara nearby. It then gives a

St Patrick makes his way to Tara.

highly fanciful account of his subsequent duel with King Laoghaire's druids, each conjuring up earthquakes, hailstones and fire. Finally St Patrick is reported to have lifted the chief druid into the air, then let him crash down "frozen solid with hail, mixed with sparks of fire". After that King Laoghaire apparently allowed St Patrick to continue his mission.

St Patrick is said to have founded several churches in King Laoghaire's kingdom though he never succeeded in converting the pagan king himself. Numerous saints after him continued to spread the gospels. Several of their so called "houses" or tiny drystone oratories survive; **St Columb's House** at Kells, **St Mochta's House** in Louth, **St Mel's Cathedral** at **Ardagh**, **St Fechin's Church** at **Fore**, and **St Ciarán's Temple** at the famous monastic settlement at **Clonmacnoise** on the banks of the Shannon (the furthest western point of the Middle Kingdom's reach). A few centuries later, when Europe was in turmoil after the collapse of the Roman Empire, there was an extraordinary flowering of Irish sculptural art. The supreme examples are in the High Crosses still preserved at **Monasterboice**, just north of Drogheda and at **Kells**. But there are examples scattered all across present day Meath and Westmeath. Alongside these early oratories and high crosses, Irish monks built round towers which served as belltowers, landmarks and lookout posts. These seem to have been inspired by the round towers in Ravenna in Italy (in turn copied from Moslem minarets) where there were two important Irish monasteries. Irish round towers were prestigious and showed remarkable building skills but they often proved easy targets for attack. One at Slane was burnt by Danish marauders along with its abbot and several monks quite soon after it was built. But there are fine surviving towers still at **Kells, Donaghmore** and **Monasterboice.** The 9th to 11th century mark a golden age for Irish art and workmanship, including the illuminated manuscripts made by

Ruins of Mellifont Abbey. FRANCIS GROSE, FROM *THE ANTIQUITIES OF IRELAND*, 1791

Irish scribes. The most famous of these is the Book of Kells, now on display in Trinity College, Dublin, but several others survive, just as fine.

As Viking raids receded, Irish monasteries were brought back under the more formal rule of the Roman Church. In 1142 St Malachy brought four disciples to the Cistercian mother house at Clairvaux in France. They returned with him to found the first Irish Cistercian abbey at **Mellifont.** From there the Cistercian monks spread to **Bective** a few miles higher up the Boyne. St Malachy also brought the Augustinian order to Ireland. Augustinian abbeys were set up at **Trim, Duleek, Clonard,** and **Kells** and even on a remote island. **Saints Island** on Lough Ree.

When the Normans arrived 30 years later, they were pleased to find offshoots of the European monastic orders already in place, and often rebuilt them in the latest Norman Gothic style. And in many respects, the Norman rule did not bring drastic changes. Meath was already almost feudal under its tribal kings. Hugh de Lacy encouraged the peasants to work their holdings as before and Gaelic leaders who accepted de Lacy's lordship usually kept part of their land. Those who did not were outlawed or often killed. The King of Breffney who came to parley with De Lacy on the **Hill of Ward** ended with his head on a spike at Dublin Castle. And much of the richest land was allotted to De Lacy's barons who in turn divided it between their followers or knights. De Lacy was a man of demonic energy and drive. He made his chief stronghold at **Trim** at a bend in the Boyne river building Ireland's largest castle, and founded two towns (later combined as **Drogheda**) on the Boyne estuary to oversee its trade. In 1181, he married the daughter of Rory O'Connor, the deposed High King without asking permission from Henry II who now suspected him of planning to seize the sovereignty of Ireland for himself. He was recalled but sent back the following winter as indispensable. In 1185, Henry sent his third son, John to Ireland as its official Lord: John complained to his father that De Lacy would not permit the Gaelic nobles to pay him tribute. In fact, the teenage prince had mortally insulted them on his first arrival by laughing and pulling at their beards. De Lacy was once again in disgrace, but remained in Ireland building castles. Gerald of Wales, the Norman historian, described him thus: "His eyes were black and deep, and his nose somewhat flat like that of an ape...his neck was short and his body hairy...but sinewish and strong.... In all public affairs he was most vigilant and careful...(but) he was very greedy and covetous of wealth and possessions". He met his end in 1186 bending over to supervise construction of a new castle at Durrow. A workman, infuriated by de Lacy's despoiling of St Columb's abbey to provide the stone, hacked off his head with one blow. When his corpse was finally retrieved, the body was taken to **Bective Abbey** for burial, the head to St Thomas's Church in Dublin. Henry II is reported not to have been displeased at the news of his death.

In the following centuries, most of de Lacy's barons consolidated their territories and built their own stone castles. Some survive as the core of later houses (such as **Dunsany** or **Barmeath**, which are still owned by the descendants of the original Norman lords) but most are now ruinous. In the 14th century, the kingdom was hit by two disasters – in 1317 Edward Bruce, brother of Robert, invaded from Scotland and ravaged the countryside, burning and sacking monasteries and towns before he was finally defeated by the Normans. Thirty years later, the Black Death arrived at Irish ports. Coastal Meath was especially badly hit, hence perhaps the numerous cadaver tombs still found there. (**St Peter's graveyard** in Drogheda has one gruesome example.) By the early 15th century, Norman rule in Meath had grown so weak that Henry IV, who was busy fighting elsewhere, offered £10 to any of his subjects who would build a tower 6m by 4.8m to defend it. (**Donore**, at Ballivor is one surviving example.) A massive ditch or Pale was built from Dundalk to Kells and south to Clonard as a further defence. Areas to the west were already half abandoned as "beyond the Pale" and outpost monasteries such as **Fore** or **Multyfarnham** were under repeated attack. Within the Pale, the Norman colony enjoyed a brief golden age in the later 15th century, and built many handsome new churches and priories. The Plunkett churches at **Rathmore** and **Dunsany** are two fine examples. Soon after however, all was to be changed by Henry VIII's break with the Pope in Rome who had refused (for political reasons) to grant him a divorce from Catherine of Aragon. In 1537 he issued a decree for the dissolution of Irish monasteries along with those in Britain and the confiscation of their lands. In most cases, Church lands in Ireland were awarded to Henry's civil servants.

In 1543, Henry VIII also divided Meath into two parts, creating East Meath and West Meath where he acknowledged "the King's writ, for lack of administration of justice, has not of late been obeyed". Twenty six years later, his daughter, Queen Elizabeth, ordered a further division, Western Meath was split into two counties, Westmeath and Longford. Meath's coastal plain had already been made part of Louth.

By the end of the 16th century, the Tudor reconquest of Ireland was almost complete. In 1603 the so-called "flight of the Earls" from Ulster gave James I the chance for a further "plantation". He appropriated their lands mainly allotting them to his fellow Scots. In 1641, dispossessed Ulster Catholics rose against them and so began the so-called Confederate Wars. They ended eight years later when Cromwell brought an army from England and ruthlessly crushed all opponents, Irish Catholics and English Royalists. Many of his soldiers were granted Irish land in lieu of pay and Catholic landowners were expelled to what they described bitterly as "a sheepwalk in Connaught". Some were allowed to return with the Restoration of Charles II, only to lose their lands again after the Williamite Wars thirty years later. The opening battle, the Battle of the Boyne took place on 1 July 1690 at **Oldbridge**, almost opposite the **Hill of Slane**, and within sight of the great Neolithic mounds of **Brú na Bóinne**, which were still quite unknown. William of Orange's army crossed the river upstream to attack the flank of James II's French and Irish troops. James fled to France abandoning them. The Jacobite army were finally defeated at Limerick the following year.

Ireland's ruling classes, and especially those in Meath, now declared themselves a Protestant nation, and passed stringent penal laws in the new Irish parliament against those who would not conform. Some of the old Catholic landowners survived by nominally handing estates over to Protestant cousins – it was their tenants and labourers who were most affected, left without churches or schools. Confident new landowners now indulged in building themselves unfortified country houses. Old tower houses were converted to barns or left as ancestral ornaments in the demesne. The leading architect, Sir Edward Lovett Pearce, from Meath, built the new Parliament house in Dublin and built Meath's grandest house, Summerhill (now sadly demolished). Only the ruins of **Arch Hall** near Wilkinstown survive in Meath to remind us of his talents.

He was followed by Richard Cassel, a German architect who changed his name to Castle. Castle specialised in the Palladian style which cleverly combined an elegant family house with wings for domestic offices and stables. **Bellinter House** near Navan is one fine example. The landscape was also being transformed; gentlemen or would be gentlemen laid out new gardens and parks, often surrounded by stone walls. Grand gates or decorative gate lodges were erected at entrances. Ornamental lakes were created by damning streams and rivers, woods were re-planted, fields were drained and given hedgerows. The most famous example of extravagant re-landscaping was at **Dangan** where Lord Mornington (grandfather of the first duke of Wellington) created a 600 acre park or garden with several artificial lakes and hills adorned with statuary in the flat Meath plains south of Trim. Not surprisingly the next generation ran

Edgeworthstown's wide main street designed for cattle fairs, with improved Georgian housing on the left, and original thatched cabins on right. FRANCIS EDGEWORTH, EARLY 1800S

out of money. But for most landowners, agricultural "improvements" made money and agricultural rents were rising fast. Many landowners also invested in new towns or villages, building handsome market houses to encourage trade, and laying out space for cattle fairs. Meanwhile the bulk of the rural population still lived at subsistence level in small thatched cabins which have long since disappeared. English and European visitors were usually shocked by their squalor, but impressed by their inhabitants' natural cheerfulness and quick wit.

For the rich, the most fashionable architect to succeed Richard Castle was Francis Johnston, from Armagh. Francis Johnston's long career spans a remarkable change in taste when Irish landowners decided that a castle would make a more impressive statement of their ancestral claims than a classical country house. Often Johnston could transform an existing house with a few well-placed towers and a row of battlements. **Tullynally** (formerly Pakenham Hall) outside Castlepollard is one example. But **Slane Castle** is probably the grandest. In 1780 its owner, the 2nd Lord Conyngham had commissioned James Wyatt from England to design flanking towers for his new mansion overlooking the Boyne. 25 years later, Francis Johnston was brought in to complete the transformation with a further array of towers and a magnificent gothick ballroom.

Recreating a castle, gothick revival additions to Pakenham Hall, Co. Westmeath.
PROPOSED BY JAMES SHEIL, 1826

In the 1820s and 30s, Johnston's brilliant pupil, James Sheil continued the process, transforming **Killua**, owned by the Chapman family, just outside Clonmellon and **Knockdrin** owned by the Levinges, 3.2km north of Mullingar. He also altered and enlarged two adjoining Norman castles owned by the Plunketts, **Dunsany** and **Killeen**.

Unlike those in England or Scotland, few of Ireland's large country houses or sham castles have survived to the present day. Anglo-Irish fortunes were often dissipated by too much time spent hunting or "travelling after pleasure" as Frederick Engels was to write indignantly to Karl Marx in 1850 when he visited Ireland after the Great Famine. ("These fellows," he added,"ought to be shot.") The effects of the Famine were at their least severe in the rich cattle ranching and tillage lands of Meath and Louth. But Westmeath lost half its population through famine, fever and emigration, and Co. Longford more than two thirds. Of the surviving landowners, many became more serious minded or evangelical: at **Castlebellingham** near Drogheda the landlord (an ardent Catholic convert) had panels with biblical inscriptions set into the facades of his new village houses and in **Ardagh** village, a widow erected an amazing pinnacled clocktower to commemorate her husband's work for the "moral and social improvement" of his tenants.

Whether the tenants preferred these moral improvers to the earlier feckless Irish foxhunting squire is another matter. The British government before and after the Famine certainly saw the failings of Irish landowners as being at the bottom of most Irish unrest. In 1903, the British Government attempted to solve the Irish Land Question for good by a bill giving tenants the right to buy out their rented lands, the government providing the necessary money to landowners in government bonds plus a cash bonus. The cash was welcome, money to repair the roof or perhaps install a bathroom or two, but the government bonds soon declined in value. Without their tenant farms, few landowners in the long run could afford to keep up a large country house. And many gave up the struggle when their heirs were killed in the First World War.

In the war of Irish Independence that followed in 1919, many country houses were burnt in retaliation for atrocities by the Black and Tans or caught

Falling into ruin, Drumcree House outside Delvin. JOHN NANKIVELL, 1960S

in crossfire of the succeeding civil war that followed. There is a moving account in Daisy Fingal's memoir, *Seventy Years Young*, of her all night vigil in one of Meath's oldest castles, **Killeen,** waiting for the "burners" to come. (It survived to be burnt 50 years later by the IRA.) In the following decade, many of the old so called Ascendancy left for England or Scotland to make new lives. The larger country houses or sham castles were sometimes bought by religious orders for schools or colleges (and often drastically altered inside and out).Some have now been returned to their former splendour as hotels or guesthouses or found new ways of supporting themselves as tourist attractions or wedding venues. But many more have become ivy clad ruins, and sometimes only a crumbling wall or a clump of old beech trees mark where they once stood. Unlike earlier historic buildings such as abbeys or medieval tower houses, which are protected by the Office of Public Works, they are not usually in the care of the State.

Yet the landscape of Meath still remains extraordinarily rich in mementoes of its past, from the great mounds and passage graves of the Neolithic age to the 20th century. You can still find superb high crosses, round towers, great medieval and gothic revival castles, ruined churches and abbeys , strange follies and gate lodges, romantic demesnes and gardens – and beautiful lakes to swim in and grassy hills to climb. Many of its attractions are still unknown to visitors. This short guide was written in the hope you will explore and discover more of Meath's original kingdom, which once stretched from the Shannon to the sea.

NB Please note that some of the places listed are only open by appointment or at certain times. Please check their websites for more information. In other cases, buildings described here are on private farmland and can only be accessed by permission. Please make every effort to obtain this to avoid trespassing or endangering stock. Irish law does not give you the right to roam.

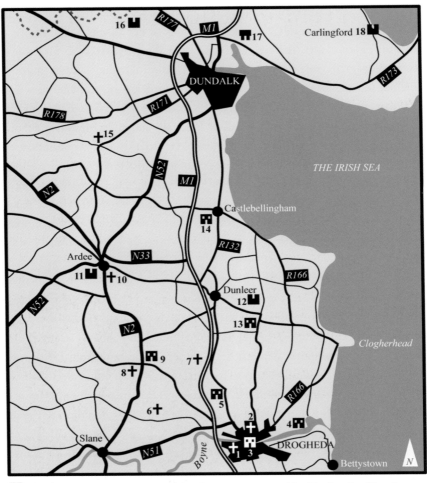

■ Castle	*1 St Mary's Church*	*10 The Jumping Church*	
▲ Cill	*2 Magdalene Tower*	*11 St Leger's Castle*	
⊓ Megalitic site	*3 The Tholsel*	*12 Barmeath Castle*	
✝ Church	*4 Beaulieu House*	*13 Rokeby Hall*	
○ Fort	*5 Killineer House & Gardens*	*14 Castlebellingham House*	
■ Entrance	*6 Mellifont Abbey*	*15 St Mary's Priory*	
⌂ House	*7 Monasterboice*	*16 Castle Roche*	
	8 Collon Church	*17 The Proleek Dolmen*	
	9 Collon House	*18 The Mint*	

in and around drogheda

Drogheda (53.7164357,-6.3794543). The name comes from Droideach Atha, Bridge of the Ford and it was an important entry point to Ireland from the earliest times. St Patrick is said to have landed here around 430AD and the Vikings established a base here for raids and trade up the river Boyne. In the 12th century, Hugh de Lacy made it the chief port for his new kingdom and built a castle on the old Viking fort. The lands to the north of the river were granted to Bertram de Verdun (whose granddaughter was to build **Castle Roche**).

Originally Hugh de Lacy founded two towns, one each side of the river. But this led to rivalry and bloodshed and in 1412, both sides agreed to seek a single charter from the King. The port's growing prosperity led to six Norman priories being built here. Now only two have visible remains, the belfry tower of **St Mary's Church** to the east and the **Magdalene tower** of the Dominican friary high up on the north side. Frequent attacks by Scots and Irish led to the town being fortified with high walls and entrance gates that closed at midnight. One of them, **St Laurence's Gate** still survives, a magnificent twin towered barbican overlooking the estuary. Having withstood numerous sieges from Scots and Irish armies, the walls of Drogheda were finally breached by Cromwell's army in September 1649, and his soldiers

The roofless nave of St Mary's church.
GEORGE PETRIE, FROM T.K. CROMWELL'S *EXCURSIONS THROUGH IRELAND*, 1821

St Laurence Gate.
HECTOR MCDONNELL

slaughtered 2,000 of its inhabitants. Hundreds more on his orders were shipped off to serve as slaves in Barbados. The massacre may have acted as a warning to others which shortened the war but it made Cromwell the most hated man in Ireland. However Drogheda recovered as a prosperous trading port with remarkable speed; it was described by one visitor in 1699 as "a handsome clean English like town, the best I have seen in Ireland". Fair Street especially has handsome merchants' houses dating from the early 18th century. One, **Barlow House**, has now become the local arts centre; and the 18th century markethouse known as the **Tholsel** (at the east end of St Laurence St) is now the town's tourist office. For a gruesome relict of the past, look in the graveyard wall of **St Peter's Parish Church** (off West Street) for the early 16th century effigy of two decomposing bodies in their shrouds. It once adorned the tomb of Sir Edmund Golding and his wife, Elizabeth Fleming (daughter of the Lord of Slane). The church itself has superb rococo plasterwork inside and a fine medieval font depicting the baptism of Christ, surrounded by angels and apostles. Since 1995 the church has also held an intricate golden shrine containing the head of St Oliver Plunkett, martyred at Tyburn in 1691, and canonised in 1975.

Drogheda north of the river, with St Peter's church far right. ANONYMOUS DRAWING, 1790S

Beaulieu House (*above*) (53.7281596,-6.297977) lies on the north bank of the Boyne, 4km east of Drogheda. The house was begun in the 1680s by a famous Royalist general, Sir Henry Tichborne who had defended Drogheda against Sir Phelim O'Neil at the start of the Confederate Wars. It was finished by his grandson in the Dutch style in the early 1700s, and is one of the earliest unfortified houses in Ireland. The **walled garden** outside is also one of the

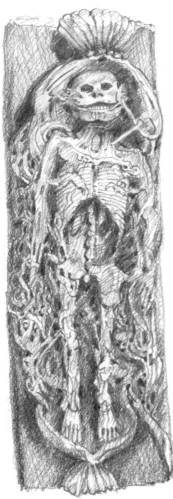

15th century cadaver tomb in church at Beaulieu.

HECTOR MCDONNELL

earliest laid out in Ireland and said to have been designed by the Dutch artist, William de Hagen. Like the house itself, it has been beautifully preserved for over 300 years by the descendants of the Tichborne family.

The adjoining church has a tomb showing a decomposing body with a snake winding its way in from one ear and out the other, one of the best preserved so-called cadaver tombs in Ireland. They seem to have been especially popular around Drogheda – see the double effigy in St Peter's graveyard and one in the Preston chapel at Stamullen. They were once common all over Europe following the Black Death which killed over half the population. The plague reached Ireland in the 1340s and was especially virulent around the coastal towns.

Accessible by appointment.

WEBSITE: *beaulieuhouse.ie*

Killineer House and Garden (53.7426319,-6.3784529) 3.7km north of Drogheda (off R132) a handsome Regency villa built for a rich Drogheda merchant, with extensive gardens laid out in the later 19th century. In front of the house formal terraces descend to a lake dotted with islands. From here paths meander through woodland gardens and a giant "laurel lawn" (once a favourite Victorian device). Dotted around are garden ornaments and statues, many of them rescued from now defunct Irish gardens. Behind the stable yard is the walled garden, still used for growing flowers, vegetables and fruit. All is superbly kept by the present owners. *Accessible by appointment.* WEBSITE: *killineerhouse.ie*

Mellifont lavabo. FRANCIS GROSE, 1790

Mellifont Abbey (53.7421577,-6.4685837) 7km northwest of Drogheda, was the first Cistercian abbey to be founded in Ireland. Its beginnings go back to 1139 when St Malachy called on his friend St Bernard at Clairvaux in France and left behind him four disciples to learn the Cistercian rule. Two years later he started to build an abbey beside the river Mattock with the help

33

of the local king. French monks, plus the four Irish disciples he had left at Clairvaux were sent over by St Bernard. The abbey's design was supervised by a Frenchman named Brother Robert and stone for decorative details was imported from Caen in Normandy. It took fifteen years to complete. Many of the French monks however returned to Clairvaux, reporting to St Bernard that the Irish monks were "wild in their rites"and "shameful in their morals".

Despite their disapproval, Mellifont flourished; by 1170 there were 100 monks and 300 lay brothers. The new Norman overlords had the church remodelled in the latest Gothic style with huge diamond-shaped piers supporting the nave and chancel. The east end of the chancel had to be literally chiselled out of rock. At the end of the cloister, there are also still parts of an octagonal lavabo (or washroom) whose magnificence (*previous page*) is said to illustrate how far the later monks departed from the original austere Cistercian rule. Water was piped into it from the nearby river through a central pillar which has long since disappeared. *Accessible all year.*

Monasterboice (53.7875125,-6.4250552) 8km northwest of Drogheda (signposted off the M1) was once the most important monastic centre in the kingdom of Meath. Still surviving are two 12th century churches, a round tower and probably the finest High Crosses in Ireland.

The most remarkable is the **Cross of Muiredach**, whose theme is Christ the King. There is a cruxifixion at the centre of the west face, and Christ ascendant in the panel above. The base of the west side has cats playing, one with a mouse, one with a bird and an inscription "Pray for Muiredach who had the Cross erected". This may refer to Muiredach who owned the land on which the monastery was built, who died about 867 AD.

The east face shows the Last Judgement with an angel with a trident pushing the bad souls away to eternal damnation. The shaft below has scenes from the Old Testament, Adam and Eve, Cain and Abel, David and Goliath, Moses striking water from the rock.

Almost as wonderfully preserved is the **West** or **Tall Cross** just in front of the Round Tower. At over 7m high, it is the tallest in Ireland. Like Muiredach's cross, it has scenes from the Old and New Testaments, and an unusually vivid

Collon Parish church, designed by the rector, Daniel Augustus Beaufort.
WATERCOLOUR BY HIS DAUGHTER, LOUISA BEAUFORT, EARLY 1800S

two-storey house in 1740 by Anthony Foster, Chief Baron of the Exchequer, it was added to by his famous son, John "Speaker" Foster, the last Speaker of the Irish House of Commons, later created Lord Oriel, who devoted his retirement to collecting rare plants. The house is now a highly rated guesthouse and the gardens have been imaginatively restored by its new owners with a parterre and topiary and superb herbaceous borders glowing with colour all summer long. *Accessible by appointment.* WEBSITE: *collonhouse.com*

The Jumping Church, Kildemock (53.8377691,-6.5281347). Ruins of a 14th century church, 3km south of Ardee. (From Collon turn right at the crossroads just after the Hunterstown Inn). The west gable of the church (which was already a ruin) is said to have jumped away from its foundations on Candlemas Day 1715 to exclude a grave of a excommunicated Catholic who had just been buried there. An unlikely story, but archeologists in the 1950s found the wall was at least 0.6m away from its original foundations, making it a mystery that it still stands up. There are good views from here towards the Mourne mountains and Carlingford Lough,

37

St Leger's Castle – the largest fortified townhouse in Ireland. HECTOR MCDONNELL

Ardee (53.8576219,-6.5487557) A garrison town established by the Normans with two fine medieval tower houses. The largest, **St Leger's Castle** at the south end of the main street is the largest fortified town house to survive in Ireland, with a battlemented walkway on the roof and a murder hole above the original entrance on the northwest side. It was later used as a courthouse and jail. **Hatch's Castle**, further along is smaller, only 3 storeys high, and was given large windows in the 18th century to make it more liveable. It was given to the Hatch family by Cromwell, and is still lived in as a private house.

Barmeath Castle, Dunleer (53.8269863,-6.3396518), has been home of the Bellews since the 12th century. There is a medieval tower house embedded inside the existing building, but most of the towers and turrets date from the 1830s, when the newly enobled Lord Bellew decided to turn his comfortable Georgian house into a Norman castle. (He has been described as replacing "good sense with wild baronial fantasy.") He commissioned them from an

St Mochta's House or oratory. HECTOR MCDONNELL

Louth Village, southeast of Dundalk (take exit 16 off M1) has the impressive ruins of **St Mary's Priory**, probably the longest priory church in Ireland. It dates from the late 13th century, and was built on the site of a much earlier monastic settlement, founded by St Mochta, a disciple of St Patrick. The only survival from this is **St Mochta's House,** (53.9533989,-6.5483996) a tiny stone roofed oratory set in the field beside the priory. It is said to have once held the saint's bones and other holy relics.

Castle Roche (54.0496561,-6.4949227) (near Kilcurry, exit 17 off M1) Making a stunning silhouette against the sky line, this was one of the largest frontier castles of the Pale. Not much remains now but a huge walled enclosure, roughly triangular with battlemented walk ways all around. It had natural defences from the rock outcrop it sits on except on the eastern side which was originally guarded by a fortified gatehouse. The castle is said to have been begun in 1236 by Lady Rohenna de Verdun after her first husband's death in France. She offered her hand in marriage to whoever could complete it. But on the eve of the wedding she asked her future husband to lean out of the window to see the lands he would soon possess, then pushed him out to his death. The window is still known as the "murder window" and his ghost is said to haunt the place.

Castle Roche, the largest frontier castle of the Norman Pale. HECTOR MCDONNELL

Perhaps as a penance, Lady Rohenna went on to found an Augustinian abbey in Leicestershire in England and died there a few years later.

The Proleek Dolmen (54.037178,-6.3504353) 4.3km east of Dundalk on the west bank of the Ballymascan river. A massive Neolithic dolmen dating back to around 3,000 BC. It once contained a cremated body, probably with grave goods such as stone tools and beads. Local folklore claims the enormous capstone was carried here by the Scottish giant Para, who challenged Finn MacCool to combat. The cunning Finn poisoned the nearby river and the giant drank from it and died. The giant's grave is said to be the wedge-shaped tomb to the southeast. Legend also claims that if a visitor can land three stones on the capstone known as the Giant's Load, his or her wish will be granted and they will be married within the year.

The Proleek Dolmen.
HECTOR MCDONNELL

There is a footpath leading to it from the car park of the Ballymascanlan Hotel.

Carlingford (54.0393592,-6.1950234) A Norman defensive town, which still retains its original medieval plan and atmosphere. Hugh de Lacy built the massive castle on a rocky outcrop overlooking Lough Carlingford and King John stayed here in 1210 while pursuing de Lacy's rebellious sons. The castle was frequently attacked by Irish and Scots and by the 17th century had become completely ruinous. But repairs were begun in the late 19th century and the ruins are usually safe to explore. (Check with the local tourist office.)

There are two fine tower houses just inside the town. One, known as **The Mint** by the Tholsel gate, was built by a wealthy merchant in the early 16th century and has carved panels above the first floor window showing a man's bust, a snake and a bird framed by elaborate Celtic ornament. **Taafe's Castle** built 60 years later, is taller with overhanging battlements. Its owner, another rich merchant, was ennobled in 1661 as 1st Earl of Carlingford.

You can explore the beautiful lough itself by catching the Carlingford ferry from Greenore port just east of Carlingford and land if you wish on the Ulster shore.

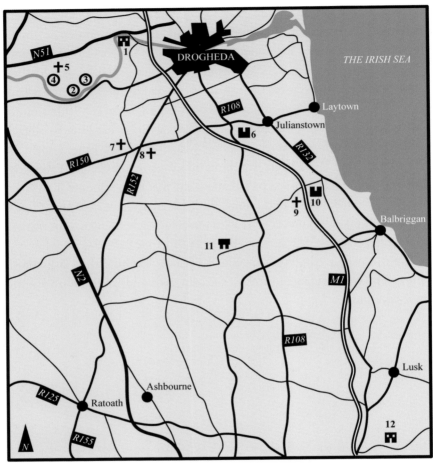

▐	Castle	**1**	Oldbridge House	**7**	St Ciaran's House
▲	Hill	**2**	Newgrange	**8**	Duleek Cross
●	Forest	**3**	Knowth	**9**	Preston Chantry chapel
✚	Church	**4**	Dowth	**10**	Gormanston Castle
○	Fort	**5**	Dowth Abbey	**11**	Fourknocks
▮▮	House	**6**	Dardistown Castle	**12**	Newbridge House
▭▭	Megalitic site				

The tumulus at Dowth, with Lord Netterville's "teahouse" on top. The teahouse was demolished 60 years later by archeologists looking for an internal chamber.
WATERCOLOUR BY GABRIEL BERANGER, 1780S

dating from 1,000 BC. There are also remains of smaller earlier passage graves, two of which have been dated to 4,000 BC. The mound itself has remains of Norman farm buildings on top – the monks of Mellifont once owned and farmed the land containing both Knowth and Newgrange.

Accessible all year. WEBSITE: *worldheritageireland.ie*

Dowth meaning the place of darkness, is the smallest and least excavated of the three great megalithic mounds of Bru na Boinne. It is possible to visit the site directly from north of the river – there is no access charge. Take the narrow country road 1km northeast of Newgrange, or follow the signpost on the road from Drogheda to Slane. Like Newgrange it is surrounded by a stone circle and one of its passage tombs is orientated to the winter solstice. Both are protected by metal grilles but you can peer inside. In the late 18th century, the reclusive owner, the 6th Lord Netterville, built himself a "teahouse" on the top of the mound from which he could follow services in the Catholic church below by telescope, having quarrelled with the local priest. It was removed in 1847 during excavations by the Royal Irish Academy to try to find a chamber inside the mound. Their dynamite blew a large hollow on the top, but without success.

To the east is the Netterville's 15th century tower house (now restored) and the redbrick **Netterville Institute** or almshouse, built with money bequeathed by Lord Netterville (who had no children) to provide for old women and orphans. His wishes, which may not always have been fulfilled, were that the inmates "should live in peace and good feeling with one another" and "be tidy, clean and perfectly sober".

Nearby are the ruins of **Dowth Abbey**.(53.7035453,-6.4497907) Nothing much is left except the walls of the long nave, but there is an interesting monument in the graveyard to John Boyle O'Reilly, whose father ran the Netterville institute school. John joined the Fenians after enlisting in the British army and was transported to Australia for treason. In 1869, he managed to escape to America (the first Irish convict to do so) and later helped organise the dramatic escape of 6 other Irish Fenians from the notorious Fremantle prison outside Perth. He rose to become the highly successful editor of the *Boston Globe* but was never able to return to the Boyne valley he loved. His bust is flanked with the allegorical figures of Ireland and America; Ireland holds a wolf hound, a sword and a flag with shamrocks and harps, America holds a flag with stars and stripes and a Bill of Freedom. O'Reilly is said to have coined the phrase "It is better to be Irish than to be right".

Dardistown Castle (53.6645112,-6.3158852), Julianstown (south of Drogheda), probably began as a "£10 castle" built in the 14th century to claim the grant from Henry VI for a towerhouse to defend the Pale. It was extended in the 16th century by Dame Jenet Sarsfield, widow of Robert Plunkett, 5th Lord Dunsany and Sir John Plunkett of Dunsoghly Castle, Dublin. The battle of Julianstown 1641 in the Confederate Wars is said to have taken place on its lawn.

More extensions were added in the 18th and 19th centuries making it a substantial country house. You can view the original castle with its vaulted rooms and sometimes climb the stairs onto its roof. There are 2 self-contained cottages to rent in the large courtyard behind the house and the upper rooms of the castle itself are also sometimes available to rent.

Accessible by appointment. WEBSITE: *dardistowncastle.ie*

Monument to John Boyle O'Reilly, editor of the Boston Globe. *Ireland is symbolised by the figure with greyhound on the left, America on the right.* HECTOR MCDONNELL

9th century cross at Duleek carved from a single piece of stone. HECTOR MCDONNELL

Duleek (53.6547493.-6.43093) – set around a village green, beside the river Nanny, this is said to be the place where St Patrick built his first stone church for St Ciarán whom he had adopted as his son. (Not to be confused with the later St Ciarán who founded Clonmacnoise). The small limestone chapel in the field north of the village is said to be **St Ciarán's house**, but is probably a late medieval oratory.

In the 12th century, an **Augustinian priory** was built here. Not much remains except the belfry tower of its church and parts of the aisle, but there is a medieval tomb chest in the aisle, showing a Crucifixion flanked by angels and saints, and another half finished tomb of a 17th century bishop of Meath, James Cusack.

But the village's star attraction is the **Duleek Cross**, north of the old parish church (which is now a ruin). Carved from a single piece of stone, it shows the Annunciation, the Visitation and the Holy Family on its shaft, and has apostles and winged beasts carved on its arms, all interspersed with elaborate Celtic decoration. It probably dates from the 9th century. And at the western end of the village don't miss a charming **wayside cross** carved with figures of angels and saints, placed there by Janet Dowdall in memory of her first husband, Thomas Bathe of Athcarne in 1601. She was a great woman for memorial crosses. She erected another for her second husband, Oliver Plunkett on a hillside beside Slane.

Stamullen, near Duleek. Look for the ruined 15th century parish church set on a small grassy hill in the centre of the village. Adjoining it is the **Preston Chantry** chapel, burial place of the Prestons of **Gormanston Castle**, which has two fine altar tombs inside. One has the life size effigy of a young woman; her shroud is tied back at her head and feet to show her decomposing body. Like the cadaver tomb in the church at Beaulieu, it probably dates from the time of the Black Death.

The second tomb dates from 1540 and has the effigy of William Preston, 2nd Lord Gormanston and his wife, Eleanor Dowdall. The lord is clad in an unusual suit of "white armour" with heavily protected shoulders, elbows and knees. (He has been compared to an American footballer!) His wife wears a jewelled cap set on a spotted veil and a tightly bodiced dress with skirts gathered to show a pleated underskirt. Imps (or angels) pluck at the cushions under both figures' heads.

The Prestons once lived at **Gormanston Castle** (53.6340026,-6.2395102) 2km to the east, now a Franciscan college. They had forfeited their lands after the Williamite Wars, but in the 1790s, George III restored the family

16th century tomb of William Preston, 2nd Lord Gormanston, and his wife in the Chantry chapel, Stamullen. HECTOR MCDONNELL

Gormanston Castle.
FROM J.P. NEALE'S *VIEWS OF SEATS*, 1823

estates as a gesture of goodwill after the dramatic rescue of the young heir from France. To celebrate, they had their house rebuilt as a vast Gothic revival castle (now rather spoilt by modern additions to the sides.) In the late 1940s, Evelyn Waugh was tempted to buy it, but then discovered to his horror that there was a Butlins holiday camp nearby.

Fourknocks (53.5965655,-6.3264915), 3km northwest of Naul, is an important late Neolithic passage grave dated around 2,500 BC. Look for the signposted path off R122. Concealed under a large grassy mound, it has an oval chamber twice the size of that at Newgrange with twelve decorated stone slabs. The one to the left of the chamber is said to show a stylised smiling human face. Over 60 skeletons were discovered inside the mound, plus numerous grave goods such as stone beads and a stone axe. The tomb is kept locked by an iron gate, but there is usually a notice stating where to find the key.
WEBSITE: *discoverboynevalley.ie/boynevalley-drive/heritagesites/fourknocks*

Neolithic stone found at Four Knocks, believed to depict a human face.
HECTOR MCDONNELL

Newbridge House (53.4866405,-6.1701993) is outside Donabate, a few km to the south. In 1744, Charles Cobbe, the new Archbishop of Dublin commissioned the celebrated English architect, James Gibbs to build him a grand classical villa here beside the sea. It took nearly ten years to complete and the Archbishop then gave it to his newly married son. The young couple filled it with pictures, fine porcelain and furniture, much of it ordered from the best Dublin painters and craftsmen. The house is now owned by Fingal Co. Council, but the family collection is still in place and the rooms furnished much as they were 200 years ago. The red drawing room is one of the grandest rooms in Ireland.

19th century watercolour of Newbridge House, Donabate.

Outside, there is a 18th century walled garden, a delightful pet farm for children, and a café and gift shop in the courtyard behind the house. The Victorian croquet lawn to the side of the house is another period piece: croquet is said to have been invented in Ireland, and the Cobbes were champion players. *Accessible all year.* WEBSITE: *newbridgehouseandfarm.com*

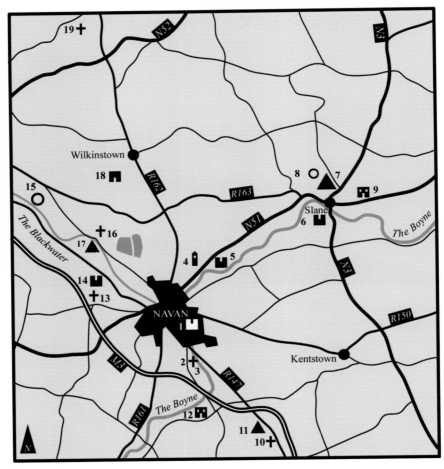

◨	Castle	1	Athlumney Castle
▲	Hill	2	Kilcarn Bridge
●	Forest	3	Church of the Nativity
+	Church	4	Donaghmore
○	Fort	5	Dunmoe Castle
◧	Entrance	6	Slane Castle
⌂	House	7	The Hill of Slane
▯	Round tower	8	Burial place of Slanius

9	Francis Ledwidge Museum
10	St Patrick's Church
11	Hill of Tara
12	Bellinter House
13	Ardbraccan Church
14	Liscarton Castle
15	Teltown
16	Donaghpatrick
17	Rath Airthur
18	Arch Hall
19	Cruisetown

58

in and around navan

Navan (53.647967,-6.7176781) began as a Norman stronghold at the junction of the river Blackwater and the Boyne. Hugh de Lacy granted the barony to Jocelyn de Angulo who built a fort here from which the town developed. The medieval walled town consisted of three streets, Trimgate Street, Watergate Street and Ludlow Street (once Dublingate Street). By the 18th century, it was thriving thanks to water power from the two rivers, with numerous corn mills and distilleries and in 1910 it replaced Trim as the county town.

One of its few surviving medieval buildings is **Athlumney Castle**, (53.6502851,-6.6773278) southeast of the town centre in Convent Road.

Ruins of Athlumney Castle. WATERCOLOUR BY GABRIEL BERANGER, 1780S

Once overlooking a bend in the river but now surrounded by modern housing, this is a 15th century tower house, with a large Jacobean manor house attached, the latter clearly designed for comfort rather than defence. It was hardly finished however when it was caught up in the Williamite Wars and its owner, Sir Lancelot Dowdall, an ardent supporter of James II, vowed to burn his house rather than let any of William's army enjoy its comforts. He set fire to it the night after the Battle of the Boyne and is said to have crossed the river to watch it burn. He then took the boat to France, never to return. It has now been partly restored and a key to the castle is usually available at Pat Boylan's guesthouse next door.

WEBSITE: *stay@athlumneymanor.com*

Kilcarn bridge (53.6324444,-6.6743717), 2.5km upstream from Navan (visible from the main Navan-Dublin road) is one of the grandest medieval bridges in Meath. Originally 4m wide, it was widened under the Turnpike Act of 1827 and now has eleven arches. In the 1980s it was threatened with demolition but saved by mass protests from the local community. It is now retired from service and used by local walkers while a concrete modern bridge takes the traffic.

Just beside it, are the ruins of Kilcarn Church, which once held a beautiful medieval font. The font was buried for safety during the Confederate and Williamite Wars and is now housed in the Catholic **Church of the Nativity** at Johnstown, on the east bank of the Boyne. The church itself is well worth a visit for its remarkable floor to ceiling stained glass windows made by Dublin artist, George Walsh in 1999. The church is normally open all day.

Donaghmore (*opposite*) An important early monastic site. 2km northeast of Navan in the old Blackcastle demesne, the original church was given by St Patrick to St Cassanus whose relics were later said to work great miracles. It was plundered and partly destroyed by the Danes in 854 and later rebuilt as a parish church (now also ruined). The surviving **round tower** is 33m high and has a Romanesque doorway 4m above ground, highly unusual for having a crucifixion carved above it, and two heads, said to represent the crucified thieves, to each side. On private farmland. *Accessible by request.*

The Church & Tower at *DONAGHMORE*. ½ M from *Navan* Co of *Meath*.

Dunmoe Castle (53.6739901,-6.67395195) (*see page 62*), downstream from Navan, is set on a spectacular site above the Boyne. For the best view, cross to the south bank of the river and look across at it from the graveyard of **Ardmulchan Church.** It was probably built by Hugh de Lacy, who later passed it to his fellow Normans, the D'Arcys. During the Confederate Wars, Dunmoe was captured by the Irish army, then attacked by Cromwell's army from across the river. After the Restoration, the D'Arcy family were re-instated as "innocent Papists". In 1688, the owner is said to have entertained James II the night before the Battle of the Boyne and the victorious William of Orange the night after. He is remembered in the mocking couplet:

Who will be King I do not know,
But I will be D'Arcy of Dunmoe.

The D'Arcys managed in fact to keep Dunmoe for the next hundred years till the castle was destroyed by fire during the Battle of Tara Hill in

Dunmoe Castle, already abandoned. DRAWN BY GEORGE PETRIE, 1830S

1798. Fifty years later, Sir William Wilde reported sadly that the family chapel was now "a filthy dungeon...strewn with the bones and coffins of this once noble family".

Slane Castle (53.7095833,-6.5636317) is set on another spectacular site above the Boyne. The original castle was built by the Flemings who lost their estate after the Confederate Wars. The land was bought by a successful Williamite General, Henry Conyngham, who built a new house here. His grandson, a noted antiquarian, brought in three famous architects in turn to gothicise it from the late 18th century, James Wyatt, James Gandon and Francis Johnston. The last of these created the spectacular round Gothick ballroom

Gateway to Slane Castle, designed by Francis Johnston. HECTOR MCDONNELL

Slane Castle. The slope below the castle has been used for pop concerts since the 1970s.
PAINTED BY THOMAS ROBERTS IN 1773

in preparation for a visit by George IV in 1821. Lady Conyngham was the king's current mistress and her complacent husband had recently been elevated to Marquis. The road from Dublin to Slane is said to have been specially straightened in order to make the king's journey to visit her easier.

Francis Johnstown also designed the two fine **gothick gate lodges**, one now the entrance to a new whiskey distillery.

Since the 1970s, Slane has been famous as a venue for pop concerts, held on the slope below the castle. Bob Dylan, the Rolling Stones, Bruce Springsteen and U2 have all played here to vast audiences. The castle has a restaurant and is open for guided tours and weddings.

WEBSITE: *slanecastle.ie*

Inside the town, don't miss the handsome square (or octagon) with four identical Georgian houses facing each other, said to have been erected for four Conyngham sisters, so that they could watch each other jealously; or the fine **medieval bridge**, 152m long, across the Boyne. On the opposite bank is a huge five-storey **corn mill,** now abandoned. It was built in 1766, mostly with money provided by Townley Balfour of neighbouring Townley Hall, and had an ingenious system for lifting corn to the upper storeys by a water wheel.

The Hill of Slane (53.7145092,-6.5480948) overlooks the town. A ring barrow on the western side, is said to mark the **burial place of Slanius or Slaine mac Dela** the first king of Meath. Later the hill became famous as the place where St Patrick lit his Paschal fire in 432 AD in defiance of the High King, Loaghaire, who was about to light the fire for the pagan Spring festival at Tara. The 7th century Life of St Patrick relates that the enraged Loaghaire set off with his druids and warriors in 24 chariots to kill the saint but they were beaten back by St Patrick, creating an earthquake and engulfing them in darkness. **St Patrick's Well** (now dried up) is still marked on the hill.

Crowning the hill are the remains of the **Franciscan monastery** and **church tower** built in the early 16th century by the Flemings, the medieval Lords of Slane. It replaced an earlier monastic building, **St Erc's Hermitage** set in the wooded grounds of Slane Castle itself. This was inhabited as late as 1530 when the two remaining hermits were finally persuaded by the Flemings to move to the new abbey. St Erc was originally a druid and said to have been one of St Patrick's earliest converts, and later appointed by him as the 1st bishop of Slane. According to folklore, he lived to the age of 90 and spent several hours a day up to his armpits in the Boyne reciting psalms, before returning to eat a frugal supper of goose eggs and three sprigs of watercress! The ruined "mortuary house" in the graveyard here is said to have once been his shrine.

The Francis Ledwidge Museum (53.7071243,-6.5296878) 2km east of Slane is the birthplace of the first world war poet, Frances Ledwidge. His father, a poor agricultural labourer, died shortly after his birth in 1887, but his mother contrived to give her nine children a happy life in this small cottage which is reflected in Francis Ledwidge's poetry, as was his passion for the surrounding countryside. From the age of fourteen, he was working on the roads, but sent some of his poems to Lord Dunsany, already a well-known writer. (*See Dunsany Castle.*) Dunsany recognised his extraordinary talent and introduced him to W.B.Yeats and other literary figures. In 1914, Ledwidge encouraged by Dunsany, enlisted in the British army, but he was also a close friend of Thomas McDonagh, one of the leaders of the Easter Rising and one of his most famous poems, the Blackbird, is a lament for his friend. A year later aged 29, he was blown up by a shell at the battle of Ypres.

The cottage was bought by a local committee and set up as a small museum in 1982 with panels depicting the story of the poet's life. It is still run by local volunteers. WEBSITE: *francisledwidge.com*

Tara (53.5788114,-6.6138377) 9km south of Navan. This beautiful hill is central to Irish mythology and from the 1st century AD replaced the Hill of Uisneach as the chief meeting place for tribal leaders and assorted kings. They would come here to discuss alliances and points of law, to feast and listen to music and long bardic recitals and when necessary to select the next High King or Ard Rí who would then undergo a ritual marriage to Maedh, the earth goddess. The druids held a great fire festival here to celebrate the spring, and it was this that St Patrick challenged when he lit his fire at Easter on the hill of Slane. According to the 7th century Life of St Patrick, the saint came the next day to Tara to dispute with King Laoghaire's druids in person and challenge their magic powers. One of the stones in the graveyard of **St Patrick's Church** is said to be the druid he froze to stone.

Tara has legends galore but needs directions to understand its history. The hill is covered with

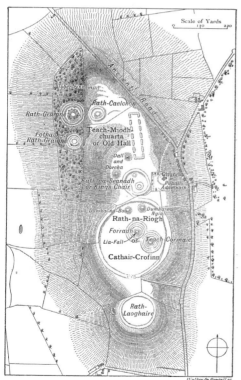

Plan of mounds on the hill of Tara.

humps and hollows which are confusing to follow. Luckily there is now a small **visitor centre** in St Patrick's Church at the eastern end of the hill to help. If it is closed, don't despair, there is a bookshop next to the car park, full of maps and guidebooks – plus an excellent café.

Inside the church, admire the wonderful stained window designed by Evie Hone to mark the 1,500th year of St Patrick's arrival. Outside there is a rather less inspiring modern statue of the saint. From here start your visit at the so-called **Banqueting Hall** to the right of the church: this consists of two parallel banks over 200m in length. In fact it is almost certainly a ceremonial entrance or cursus dating from Neolithic times. Once through the passage you come to the **Mound of the Synods**, so called because it was here the Irish churchmen met here in early Christian times to rewrite the laws of Ireland. At the final synod, St Ruadan cursed Tara "May Tara be desolate for ever" – the only way it seems pagan worship of such an iconic site could be stopped.

In the early 20th century, the Mound of the Synods was badly vandalised by British Israelites searching for the Ark of the Covenant! They are said to have been encouraged by their landlord, Gussy Briscoe with whom they were staying as paying guests at **Bellinter House** nearby. He buried a series of wooden boxes there for them to discover. They were finally driven off the hill by indignant protesters, including W.B. Yeats and Maud Gonne. The mound was re-excavated properly in the 1950s and a number of Roman coins and other artefacts were found, showing connections between Tara and the Roman world.

Beyond it is a huge circular earthwork known as the **Enclosure of the Kings** and inside this is the so-called **Mound of the Hostages**, in fact a Neolithic passage grave dating back to 3,200BC. Originally this was a communal grave holding hundreds of cremated bones, but it was later used in the Bronze Age as a burial place for the elite. The last burial was of a young man with an ornate necklace of bronze and amber and jet.

Beside it forming a kind of figure of eight are two smaller mounds: one is **Teach Chormaic,** said to be home to the legendary King Cormac Mac Art (father of Gráinne who eloped with Diarmuid) and another the **Forradh** or Royal Seat. And on top of the Forradh is an ancient phallic stone known as the **Lia Fail**, the

Stone of Destiny. It was said to give out a roar when the rightful High King touched it. Apparently, the roar was produced by driving chariot wheels hard against it.

Another stone pillar beside it commemorates the bloody **Battle of Tara Hill**, fought here in 1798 between the United Irishmen and a local yeomanry force led by Lord Fingal. The United Irishmen far outnumbered the yeomanry but were poorly armed with pikes and scythes and pitchforks while the other side had well-disciplined cavalry and cannon. Over 400 "rebels" were killed before they fled. They were buried here in a mass grave.

Tara continued to be a rallying point for Irish nationalists long after. In 1843 Daniel O'Connell held one of his "monster meetings" here to call for the abolition of the Union with England and nearly a million people attended. In the 1940s

Lia Fail or the Stone of Destiny, Tara.
HECTOR MCDONNELL

Tara was proposed as the neutral capital of a united Ireland and an architect even drew up plans for a new city here with parliament, cathedral, university and airport. Luckily the "curse" of Tara has remained and its green hill has been left "desolate" enough to be grazed by sheep, disturbed only by hundreds of walkers and the occasional archaeological dig. *Accessible all year.*

Bellinter House (53.5980812,-6.6645867), 3km from Tara is an elegant Palladian mansion designed by Richard Castle for a rich brewer, John Preston,

Bellinter House, now a boutique hotel and spa. HECTOR MCDONNELL

Rococo plasterwork in Bellinter House. PHOTO: ROBERT O'BYRNE

who later became Lord Tara, taking his name from the famous hill. In the early 20th century it was owned by a boisterous hunting squire, Gussie Bristow (*see Tara*) who encouraged the British Israelites to stay here as paying guests while they searched his land at Tara for the Ark of the Covenant (*see the Mound of the Synod*) in order to raise money for his hunt. The house was saved from dereliction after his death by being bought by nuns. It has since been sold and has now been converted to a comfortable boutique hotel with a spa in one wing.

WEBSITE: *bellinterhouse.com*

Just south of the bridge over the Boyne, look for Riverstown Castle, a massive square tower built by the Dillons whose tomb can be seen in the ruined parish church of Newtown Trim (*p. 76*).

Ardbraccan just south of Navan, was once the seat for the Bishops of Meath. The bishop's palace is still privately owned and not accessible. But it is worth visiting the handsome classical church in woodland southeast of the house which has a freestanding medieval tower crowned with an 18th century spire.

Look for the monument in the graveyard to an early bishop of Meath, George Montgomery, rather crudely depicted on it with his wife and daughter. In fact he was seldom here and spent most of his time at court in London as chaplain to James I. At the back of the monument a plaque commemorates a later bishop, the famous eccentric traveller, Richard Pococke, who was buried here in 1765. Pococke planted two cedars of Lebanon in the churchyard, with seeds he had brought back from his travels but sadly they have not survived.

Liscarton 3km upstream from Navan beside the Blackwater has two ruined castles built by the Talbots in the early 15th century and a ruined church. The church has mullioned windows with perfect late gothic tracery and the carved heads of a King, Queen and Bishop projecting from the dripstones outside. From the mid 19th century the castles were owned and lived in by the Cullen family (brothers of the famous Cardinal Cullen) who operated a prosperous mill here, hence the long range of farm buildings. They finally sold the land in 1963. On private farmland. *Accessible by request.*

Teltown Halfway between Kells and Navan, Teltown is the ancient site of the Tailtean games, held here in pagan times. These were a kind of Olympic games, with horse and chariot races, running, wrestling and other feats of strength and took place every year on 1 August until the time of the last High King. Also held here were the so-called Tailtean betrothals. Young men were separated from girls by a high wall and had to choose their bride unseen from her finger poked through a hole in a wooden door. If the couple did not get on, they could return the following year to have their marriage dissolved and try again. "What a pity", wrote Sir William Wilde in 1849, "there is no Teltown marriage in the present day. What numbers would take advantage of it."

St Patrick is said to have visited Teltown early on in his missionary travels and converted Conall, King Loaghaire's brother, who then offered him his royal rath for a church. According to legend, a furious King Loaghaire came here to prevent this and St Patrick had the king confined to a dark hole beside the river Blackwater as "a short road to hell". Centuries later, Wilde relates, some locals went to cut turf from this spot and "had barely lifted the scraw in the hollow before a terrible roaring was heard...and presently a most venomous

Rath Airthur, now planted with trees.
HECTOR MCDONNELL

serpent with a huge mane and a head as big as a horse, rose up out of the pit and looked about him." Not surprisingly the turf cutters fled.

St Patrick is said to have built his church at **Donaghpatrick** just to the east, where the present parish church now stands. Opposite it is an enormous mound, 10m high, known as **Rath Airthur,** which may have been the site of Conall's original dwelling. It has been planted with trees, but you can still trace the three lines of embankments around the rath on the summit. *Accessible by request.*

North of Navan, it is worth seeking out **Arch Hall**, a fascinating early 18th century ruin outside Wilkinstown. The place takes its name from the elaborate archway made of eroded stones that once framed the avenue to the house. (The avenue has long been cut down, leaving only a flat field in between). Both were probably designed around 1730 by Meath's most famous architect, Sir Edward Lovett Pearce. The house was one room deep with domed circular rooms at each end of the ground floor where bits of the original plasterwork can still be seen. It was built for the Payne family. *Accessible by request.*

Arch hall entrance gate framing the ruined house behind. HECTOR MCDONNELL

Further north again on the R162, make for **Nobber village** (just off the map) the birthplace of the famous blind harpist Carolan, the last of the Irish bards. Just north (still on R162) is one of Hugh de Lacy's most massive mottes which later became a crucial stronghold for Royalist forces during the Confederate Wars. In the village itself, look for the ivy covered remnants of a medieval church tower and built into a wall beside it the upright effigies of Gerald Cruise and his wife, Margaret Plunkett, dating from the early 15th century. 3km southwest is the more complete church at **Cruisetown** with a monument to two later Cruises, Walter and his wife Elizabeth, erected by their son Patrick in 1680. The doll-like figures have a band of cherubs hovering above their heads. In the graveyard is a large limestone cross, obviously inspired by the early Irish high crosses with a naïve crucifixion on one side and a Virgin holding a hefty child Jesus on the other.

17th century monument to Walter and Elizabeth Cruise, Cruisetown Church, erected by their son. HECTOR MCDONNELL

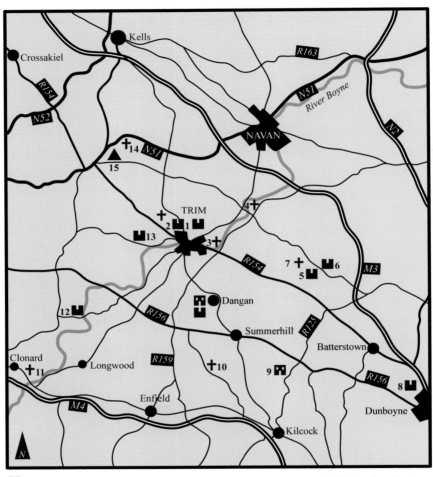

■	Castle	**1**	Trim Castle	**9** Larch Hill Arcadian Gardens
▲	Hill	**2**	Talbot's Castle	**10** Agher Church
●	Forest	**3**	Cathedral of Saint Peter & St Paul	**11** St Finnian's Church
		4	Bective Abbey	**12** Donore Castle
✝	Church	**5**	Dunsany Castle	**13** Trimblestown castle
○	Fort	**6**	Killeen Castle	**14** Rathmore Church
■	Entrance	**7**	St Nicholas' Church	**15** The Hill of Ward
▦	House	**8**	Dunboyne Castle	

in and around Trim

Trim (53.5544205,-6.791588) was once at the very centre of the Norman Pale. Set on a bend in the Boyne river, it has the largest and most spectacular **Norman castle** in Ireland. The first castle here was built of wood in 1172 by Hugh de Lacy almost as soon as he was granted the lordship of Meath by Henry II. But when he left briefly for England, it was attacked by Rory O'Connor, the deposed High King of Ireland and burnt down. De Lacy returned to rebuild it with massive towers and other defensive features and cut a ditch so the Boyne waters encircled it on all sides. There was a drawbridge and concealed stairways and booby-traps inside the 3.3m thick walls. De Lacy was killed before it was complete. When King John arrived in 1210 to claim sovereignty, de Lacy's son, Walter, defied him by locking the castle and forcing the king to camp outside. Walter then fled to Carlingford, but was later reinstated as Lord of Meath. For the next three hundred years the castle had no permanent family occupant. But it was still used for ceremonial meetings and was one of the chief garrisons of the Norman Pale. In 1399, Richard II left his two sons here as wards; one of them, Prince Hal, was to become King Henry V.

Meanwhile a medieval town had grown up beside the castle, the town walls touching the castle at its southeastern corner. **Sheepsgate** is all that remains

Trim Castle from the north, encircled by the Boyne river. HECTOR MCDONNELL

73

Trim Castle from the south, showing its fortified entrance. HECTOR MCDONNELL

of these, but the town still has its fine early medieval bridge across the Boyne.

After the Williamite Wars, Trim Castle was granted to the Wesleys (later Wellesleys) who lived at Dangan nearby. They sold it to the Plunkett family and Lord Dunsany sold it to the State in 1993. Soon after, it became famous as the filmset for *Braveheart*, and, partly reroofed, was made a tourist attraction. Excellent guided tours are now on offer during summer months or you can simply picnic in the lawns around it and admire its mighty walls.

Across the river is **Talbot's Castle**, once home to Sir John Talbot, Lord Lieutenant of Ireland, and beside it, the **Yellow Steeple**, 38m high, the ruined bell tower of St Mary's Church, burnt to save it from capture by Cromwell's army.

Open by appointment.

Talbot's Castle and the Yellow Steeple. HECTOR MCDONNELL

There is a new millennium bridge built across the Boyne to link this directly to de Lacy's castle. Talbot's Castle probably once contained the refectory of the original abbey adjoining the church. Later it became a Diocesan school and was attended by the young Arthur Wellesley living at Dangan nearby. He is said to have enjoyed his time there and at the age of 21 became the local MP for Trim. There is a magnificent Corinthian pillar carrying his statue west of the castle, erected in his honour in 1817, after his defeat of Napoleon at Waterloo.

The Duke of Wellington's pillar.
PHOTO: JOSEPH CARR

1.5km downstream at Newtown Trim is another impressive Norman ruin. You can walk to it or park your car just across the small humped bridge. This is the **Cathedral of Saint Peter and St Paul**, founded by Simon de Montfort, 1st Bishop of Meath. It was once the largest medieval church in Ireland and the nave (now only half its original size) still

The ruined Cathedral at Newtown Trim, left, with Trim Castle in the distance, right.
WATERCOLOUR BY GABRIEL BERANGER, 1780S

16th century tomb of Sir Lucas Dillon and his wife, Parish church, Newtown Trim.
HECTOR MCDONNELL

conveys a sense of its grandeur. A window at the western end perfectly frames Trim Castle across the river. Beside it are the ruins of the abbey whose friars once had charge of the cathedral. To the east there is a small medieval parish church with the 16th century tomb of Sir Lucas Dillon and his wife Lady Jane Bathe. It is known locally as the **Tomb of the Jealous Man and Woman** because a sword divides them and is said to provide a cure for warts. (Rub a pin on the wart, place it between the couple and as the pin rusts the wart will disappear.)

Heading back towards Trim, stop at the gate just opposite the Abbey, call out and the Abbey will send back a perfect echo as if still inhabited.

Bective Abbey (53.5824741,-6.705083) is a few km northeast of Trim on the north bank of the Boyne. Founded by Cistercians in 1142, this was the first "daughter "house to Mellifont Abbey. The land was given to them by Murchadh O'Melaghin, King of Meath, but they quickly became allied to the new Norman rule. In 1196 the body of Hugh de Lacy was brought here for ceremonial burial, but it was removed nine years later by papal decree to be re-united with his head at St Mary's Church in Dublin.

Ruins of Bective Abbey. FRANCIS GROSE, *ANTIQUITIES OF IRELAND,* 1791

The cloister at Bective Abbey, showing a bishop carved on one pillar.
ENGRAVING AFTER GEORGE PETRIE, T.K. CROMWELL'S *EXCURSIONS THROUGH IRELAND,* 1821

The abbey was closed in 1537 under the edict of Henry VIII but its rich lands made it a prize asset and its new owner, Thomas Agard began the process of converting it to a Tudor manor house. The cloister became an internal courtyard, the sacristy a bakehouse with a large bread oven, and the monks' dormitory above was remodelled as two large rooms with mullioned windows. The results were still so "medieval "that Bective was used as the set for Edward I's castle in the film of *Braveheart* in the 1990s. *Accessible all year.*

The restored obelisk at Dangan
HECTOR MCDONNELL

Dangan (53.5029732,-6.7604142) 5km southeast of Trim. This was once the estate of the Wesley or Wellesley family, and you can still see the ruined remains of the house where the Duke of Wellington spent his childhood. It was built by his grandfather in the 1740s who created around it an immense ornamental park or gardens of over six hundred Irish acres adorned with obelisks and statuary set among clumps of trees and artificial lakes. Archbishop Pococke described the result as the most beautiful place he had seen in Ireland. A visiting friend of the family, Mrs Delany, also described them with admiration including the toy fort on the lake where her godson Garrett Wesley (the future father of the Duke) could play "lord high admiral". But she was rather shocked at such extravagance. Sure enough, by the time her godson had grown up to become the first Lord Mornington, the Wellesleys were running out of money and in the 1790s, his son, the first Marquis of Wellesley decided to sell the place.

Soon after the house and gardens were sold, they were despoiled by a tenant, Roger O'Conor (who was also suspected of hiding United Irishmen there during the Rising of 1798). In 1809 the house was partly gutted by fire. The roofless shell still looks remarkably intact from a distance. but of the once vast gardens only two obelisks remain, one a mere stump, one recently restored by a local campaign. But the lake with its toy fort probably inspired a neighbouring squire to create the same on a smaller scale (*see Larch Hill.*)

Dunsany Castle. ENGRAVING AFTER GEORGE PETRIE,
T.K. CROMWELL'S *EXCURSIONS THROUGH IRELAND,* 1821

Dunsany Castle (53.5355937,-6.6230717) 13.9km southeast of Trim. Probably built by Hugh de Lacy in the 12th century, Dunsany has been owned by the Plunketts since the early 15th century, when Sir Christopher Plunkett married the heiress of **Killeen Castle** next door. Sir Christopher was later created Lord Fingal and by making himself useful to the King, Henry VI, was able to provide castles and estates for six of his seven sons. (The seventh became a priest.) The oldest two, according to legend, divided the Killeen lands amicably between them by getting their wives to race from opposite ends of the estate with the boundary to be set where they met. The wife starting from Dunsany ran faster and was the winner. The two families managed to remain close neighbours and friends for centuries after, the Protestant Lords Dunsany supporting the Catholic Lords Fingal during the worst of the penal times.

In the late 18th and early 19th century, thanks to a talent for marrying heiresses, both the Dunsany and Killeen Plunketts were able to upgrade their crumbling castles, doubling their original size and commissioning elegant Gothic interiors from the architect, Francis Johnston and then from his pupil, James Sheil.

In the early 20th century, Dunsany had its most remarkable owner yet. The 18th Lord Dunsany was a brilliant novelist and playwright – at one stage he had 5 plays running simultaneously on Broadway. He encouraged the young poet, Francis Ledwidge (*see the Frances Ledwidge Museum*) and introduced him to W.B.Yeats and other Irish literary figures. He was also an enthusiastic big game hunter who filled the castle with trophy heads – visitors were once greeted in the front hall by a snarling stuffed lion. The castle is now owned by his great grandson, the 21st Lord Dunsany, who has recently embarked on a "rewilding" of parts of the demesne.

Accessible by appointment. WEBSITE: *dunsany.com*

Beside the entrance drive, look for the ruins of a substantial 15th century church, **St Nicholas,** with a towerhouse attached. Inside is a beautiful octagonal font carved with pairs of the Apostles, and in a side chapel, there is a tomb with the recumbent figures of Sir Christopher and his first wife, Anne Fitzgerald. He lavished riches on the church during his lifetime and left a will commanding his children to find priests to pray for him and his two wives or to suffer "God's curse and mine".

16th century wayside cross.
ROBERT O'BYRNE

If the castle and church are not open to visitors, you can still admire the two handsome entrance gates in contrasting gothick styles. The main entrance, the so-called **Folly gate**, is a fantasy from the 1760s featuring a tower with a "crumbling" parapet and mock arrowloops. (There is a 16th century wayside cross just outside it carved with a worn crucifixion.) The **Tower gate** just beyond it was built 70 years later by James Sheil with a fake portcullis and a gothick gate lodge tucked in behind.

Killeen Castle (53.5353853,-6.5983811) just east of Dunsany, also claims to be a de Lacy castle, granted to one of his barons, Geoffrey de Cusack. In 1403, Joan Cusack, heiress to Killeen, married Christopher Plunkett of Rathmore, later created Earl of Fingal who amassed huge swathes of land for his family (*see Dunsany above*).

Killeen Castle. ENGRAVING AFTER GEORGE PETRIE,
T.K. CROMWELL'S *EXCURSIONS THROUGH IRELAND,* 1821

After the Confederate Wars the Killeen estate was forfeited for backing the wrong side, but it was returned by Charles II and the Lords Fingal remained the largest Catholic landowners in Ireland (partly owing to protection from their Protestant cousins at Dunsany.) But the castle itself was given up and by the early 18th century had become partly ruinous.

Like neighbouring Dunsany, it was rescued 50 years later when castles once again became the fashion and was enlarged and remodelled. Lord Fingal, still Catholic but now a loyal supporter of the crown, led the Yeomanry at the Battle of Tara Hill.

Like many grand houses in Meath, Killeen was threatened with burning during the Irish civil war, and Daisy, wife of the 11th Lord Fingal, in her memoir *Seventy Years Young* left a moving description of sitting up all night in 1921 waiting for the burners to come, while her husband fell asleep beside her. They never came, but the castle was sold by her son, 12th Earl in 1951, and was partly burnt 30 years later by the IRA. It was bought in 1997 by developers and is currently being restored as a luxury hotel. The parkland is now a successful golf course, and you can admire the castle from the golf club restaurant even if you do not play golf.

Accessible by appointment. WEBSITE: *killeencastle.com*

Dunboyne Castle (53.4138316,-6.4886697) on the outskirts of Dunboyne town, is not so much a castle as a splendid Palladian house. (The remains of the original castle are in a churchyard nearby). Its story is one of the oddest of Irish country houses. The Lords Dunboyne (a Catholic branch of the powerful Butler family) had lost their estates after the Williamite Wars, but in the 1760s, had recovered them by outwardly conforming to the Protestant Church. They commissioned the Drogheda architect, James Darley to design them an imposing new house. However, in 1789, the title passed to an elderly uncle who was by then the Catholic bishop of Cork. Torn between faith and what he saw as family duty, the bishop unfrocked himself and married aged 70 in the hope of producing an heir; but in vain, his only child died young. In an act of contrition he willed the house and all his lands to the Catholic college at Maynooth. The will was contested by his sister who won back the house and half the lands. Eventually the house was sold to an order of nuns. Then in the 1990s, it was re-sold and converted to a hotel. It is well worth a stop off for a meal to see the fine rococo plasterwork on the staircase and inside the main rooms.

WEBSITE: *dunboynecastlehotel.com*

Larch Hill Arcadian Gardens (53.4411683,-6.6609902) 5km from Kilcock. A fascinating ornamental farm or *ferme ornée* unique in Ireland with gothic farm buildings and beautiful shellwork in a garden tower. It was created in the mid 18th century by a squire called Robert Watson who probably took his inspiration from Lord Mornington's magnificent gardens at Dangan, a few km away. Like him, he built a lake with a toy fort at its centre. He also believed he would be re-incarnated as a fox, and built a fox's earth topped by a small temple. Farm buildings, garden and follies have been lovingly restored by the present owners.

Accessible by appointment. WEBSITE: *larchill.ie*

Agher Church (53.4543049,-6.7549546) southwest of Summerhill. The parish was once part of Jonathan Swift's living in Meath though he was

The Fox's Earth Folly at Larch Hill Arcadian Gardens. HECTOR MCDONNELL

more concerned with his church at Laracor outside Trim (now demolished). The church was rebuilt in 1804 by the Winter family and has a window painted by Thomas Jervais of St Paul preaching copied from a Raphael cartoon by Thomas Jervais. Jervais was renowned for using a special process

The Winter family's mausoleum, Agher Parish church graveyard. HECTOR MCDONNELL

of painting on glass and this is the only remaining example of his work in Ireland. The pretty church is still regularly used for services.

Beside the church, look for the **Winter family's mausoleum**, a perfect gothick building in miniature. The Winters were reported to be model early 19th century landlords housing their "numerous peasantry" in "eligible dwellings with all decency and comfort". Their house has long vanished, demolished in 1947 by the Irish Land Commission.

Clonard (53.4499923,-7.0210367) 5km east of Kinnegad on the N4. There was an important monastic settlement here founded by St Finnian in 520 AD. He set up a school and became known as "The Master of the Souls of Ireland" because so many future saints studied under him, including St Columb and St Ciaran, the founder of Clonmacnoise. The monastery was pillaged and burnt by the Danes and then by the Normans but survived till Henry VIII's Dissolution, when the monastic lands were given to Sir William Bermingham. The fine early **15th century baptismal font** survives in **St Finnian's Church** (set back from the road, just opposite the Monastery Inn.)

Its biblical scenes are still as crisp as if they were newly carved, and are brightly lit by modern stained glass windows telling the story of St Finnian's life. A north window shows an angel calling on him to found his monastery beside the Boyne. *The church is usually accessible from 11a.m. – 4 p.m.*

Donore Castle (53.4942309,-6.9438184) 10km south of Trim on R161, on the north bank of the

15th century font in St Finnian's Church, Clonard. The central panel depicts Joseph and Mary's Flight into Egypt.
HECTOR MCDONNELL

Boyne. A small defensive towerhouse still largely intact, built like Dardistown to claim the £10 grant offered by Henry VI to any of his subjects who would help to defend the Norman Pale. There is a "murder hole" above the doorway as an added defence and carved heads of a bishop and king. The staircase to the upper floors is partly ruinous and not advisable.

It was probably built by the powerful McGeoghegan clan who once owned large areas of western Meath. *(See another Donore Castle at Horseleap in Co. Westmeath)* In 1650, the castle was captured by Colonel Reynolds, a zealous Cromwellian and over 40 McGeoghegans, including women and children, are said to have been massacred by his troops. Reynolds rose to be commissioner general of the horse in Cromwell's army and later bought a large estate in Cork. Donore was occupied until the early 19th century, probably by a local farmer; a drawing of 1785 shows it with a thatched roof.

Trimblestown Castle 3km west of Trim on the banks of the Trimblestown river. Take the Kildalkey road, and turn the second right after 2.5km. There is a lane leading the castle across the fields. This massive castle dating from the early 15th century was built by the Barnewalls, one of Meath's most powerful Norman families. In 1461, a younger son was raised to the peerage as Lord Trimblestown. They were briefly exiled as Catholics after the Confederate Wars, but returned in the 1700s. Richard Lovell Edgeworth in his memoirs records the 12th Lord Trimblestown as a man of great benevolence, famous for his healing powers who gave advice and herbal medicines to the local people.

In the 1790s, the 14th Lord decided to modernise the castle, perhaps to please a much younger wife, (he was 70, she was 24). You can still see the shell of his drawing room with its new bay windows. But in the late 19th century, the castle seems to have been abandoned and fell slowly into ruin. Like many Irish ruins, it is now engulfed in ivy with saplings growing up through its towers. But the little chapel nearby, where the family was buried, has been restored by local volunteers.

Rathmore Church (53.6430556,-6.8744109) 4.5km east of Athboy. A 15th century church built by Sir Thomas Plunkett. Sir Thomas married Mary Cruise in 1432 and the armorial carvings on the altar have been described as a veritable

The ruins of Trimblestown Castle, abandoned in the late 19th century.
PHOTO: ROBERT O'BYRNE

"Who's Who of the Northern Pale" with the arms of Plunketts, Fitzgeralds, Bellews, Berminghams and Talbots. There is a fine altar tomb in the sacristy of Sir Thomas and his wife, dated 1471, his feet resting on a little dog.

The Hill of Ward (53.6244436,-6.8948659) 1.5km east of Athboy. A huge grassy mound topped with four embankments, that was once the site of an important pagan festival at the autumn solstice or Samhain (the forerunner of Christian Halloween). It was known as the hill of Tlachtga, after a druidess in Irish mythology who is said to have given birth to triplets on the hill. In 1168, the High King, Rory O'Connor, held a massive gathering at the site. Four years later, Hugh de Lacy had seized power. The king of Breffney, Tiernan O'Rourke, went up the hill to parley with him. What transpired exactly is confused, but Tiernan O'Rourke ended up dead and his head was sent to adorn a spike outside Dublin Castle.

Private land. *Accessible by permission.*

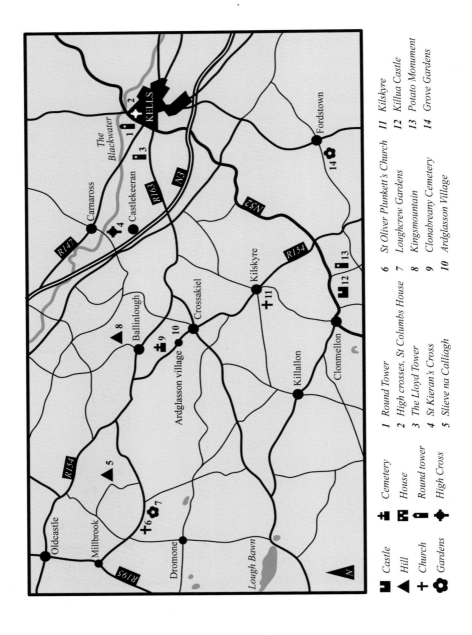

The Blackwater

KELLS

Carnaross

Castlekeeran

Fordstown

Ballinlough

Crossakiel

Kilskyre

Killallon

Clonmellon

Ardglasson village

Oldcastle

Millbrook

Dromone

Lough Bawn

R147

R163

N3

N52

R154

R195

N

1 Round Tower
2 High crosses, St Columbs House
3 The Lloyd Tower
4 St Kieran's Cross
5 Slieve na Calliagh
6 St Oliver Plunkett's Church
7 Loughcrew Gardens
8 Kingsmountain
9 Clonabreany Cemetery
10 Ardglasson Village
11 Kilskyre
12 Killua Castle
13 Potato Monument
14 Grove Gardens

✚ Cemetery
🏠 House
▬ Round tower
✛ High Cross

🏰 Castle
▲ Hill
✚ Church
✿ Gardens

88

in and around kells

Kells (53.7284579,-6.8828839) The Irish name Ceannanus Mór means Great
Residence and Kells was once a royal site: the famous High King, Cormac
MacArt (father of Gráinne) is reported to have built a palace here for his
retirement. About 560 AD, another High King Diarmuid MacCarroll granted
a site to Columb or Columcille, a prince of the northern Uí Néills, to establish a
monastery here. In the 9th century, more monks fled here from their monastery
on Iona, (also founded by Columb) to escape the Vikings, probably bringing
with them the famous illuminated manuscript now known as the Book of Kells.

The monastery suffered repeated attacks from
Viking and Irish marauders, then was taken
over by the Normans who made the place a
walled town. The town was sacked and burnt by
Edward Bruce in 1317 in his savage campaign to
become King of Ireland and much was destroyed
again during the Confederate Wars but the town
has kept its medieval street pattern.

Monastic remains are grouped around the
present Church of Ireland at the top of the town.
There are four **High Crosses** in the graveyard,
the largest of which is slightly broken at the
top. (It is said to have been used for hanging
United Irishmen during the 1798 rebellion).
Like some at Monasterboice, its sculptures seem
almost classical: the base has a frieze of mounted
soldiers that could have been made in Rome. A
fifth cross, originally in the town centre, has now
been placed outside the Courthouse for safety

The broken High Cross at Kells.
ENGRAVING FROM
GEORGE PETRIE, 1821

89

Croft or upper storey of St Columb's House. DRAWN BY WILLIAM FRAZER, 1890s

having been hit several times by passing lorries.

There is a **round tower** just outside the Church of Ireland graveyard, nearly 30m high and missing its cap. It has five windows, which would once have served as lookouts for the five ancient roads approaching the town, one from Tara.

St Columb's House, also just outside the graveyard, was probably built as an oratory like St Mochta's house in Louth. Originally it contained a large flat stone known as St Columb's bed but the relics of the saint were moved elsewhere centuries ago. The walls are immensely thick but light still shines through a window to a desk by the fireplace where the monks may have worked at their books. They would have climbed by ladder to the original doorway (now blocked up) 2.5m above the ground, and the Annals of the Four Masters reported there was also an underground passage to the church next door.

In the 1850s, William Wilde reported it inhabited by "a miserable wretched family" and an illustration in his book shows it half ruinous with a thatched roof. It has now been restored and you can usually get access on request. WEBSITE: *visitingkells.ie*)

90

The original **Book of Kells** is now on display in Trinity College in Dublin, but there is a replica in the new **Kells Heritage Centre** in the old Courthouse. A superb crozier of the same period, the Kells crozier, is now in the British Museum. Across the road from the courthouse is the cemetery of St John's with a fine crusader tomb in the far left hand corner.

The early saints could be highly competitive. **Castlekeeran (53.7342138,-6.9657596)** just west of Kells on the banks of the Blackwater river was the site of another early church, founded by St Kieran. You can still see the **High Crosses** in the four corners of the graveyard here, all with elaborate interlaced decoration. The north cross has been broken off leaving only a stump. The upper part lies close by the river; it is said to have been left here by St Columb when he was caught red-handed by St Kieran, carrying it off for his new monastery at Kells.

From the late 17th century, Kells had become the property of the Taylor family, one of the richest landowners in Meath. Their house is now a boarding school, but you can follow its walls of its great parkland for more than a mile to the east of the town. Another memorial is the 30.5m high **Lloyd Tower** (53.7329808,-6.9076712) to the west towards Oldcastle. Looking like an abandoned lighthouse, it was erected by Thomas Taylor, 1st Earl of Bective in 1794 in memory of Colonel Lloyd who had encamped here with his soldiers during the Williamite Wars. There are 164 steps to the platform at the top from which Lord Bective is said to have enjoyed watching the local hunt. The tower is now owned by the local community and you can usually climb the steps yourself for great views of the surrounding countryside. There is a small picnic area and children's playground at its base.

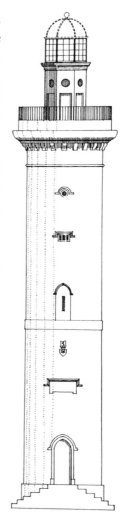

The Lloyd tower, erected 1794.

91

The Loughcrew Hills If you want to get a feel of Neolithic Ireland without the hassle and bustle of Bru na Boinne, this is the place to find it. The Loughcrew hills are a 4km long ridge just east of Oldcastle with three principal peaks, **Slieve na Calliagh** (or the Hag's mountain, 290m high), **Carnbane East** (260m) and **Carnbane West** (240m). Spread across them are 30 chambered cairns, making them one of the largest Neolithic complexes in Europe, dating from around 3,500 BC. (They are thought to predate the great mounds in the Boyne valley).

The largest cairn is on Carnbane West (60m in diameter). But the most accessible is Cairn T (53.744576,-7.1143117) on Slieve na Callaigh where there is a small car park and steps leading up the steepest part of the hill. It has huge kerbstones, one of which with a hollowed out seat is known as the **Hag's chair**. There are 27 decorated stones or orthostats. The passage to the central chamber is lit up by the sun at the autumn and spring solstice, and there is usually a local festival held here to celebrate the spring.

The cairns contained bones, ashes from cremations, and vast quantities of bone pins and ornaments, broken pottery, and stone beads, mostly from the Bronze Age, though late Iron Age glass and amber have been found too. There are wonderful views from the top across the great central plain of Meath. You can find refreshments after your climb at the Megalithic café 0.5km away. WEBSITE: *loughcrewmegalithiccentre.com*

Many of the hills still belong to the Naper family who came here in the 17th century, dispossessing the Catholic Plunketts. St Oliver Plunkett was born here (his parents are buried at **Clonabreany** nearby). He became a priest, went to work in Rome and was sent back to Ireland by the Pope to revitalise the church. But he was then arrested by the English, falsely accused of treason and hung, drawn and quartered, the last victim of the so-called Popish plot. His head is preserved in St Peter's Church in Drogheda.

The Napers at one point owned 180,000 acres of land and built an imposing classical mansion in the early 19th century facing the cairns. It was said to be cursed and was burnt down 3 times. The present owner has bravely converted the splendid stable courtyard into a wedding venue, and resurrected the portico of the original house. She has also restored the original **17th century gardens** beside **St**

Ruined 19th century portico of Loughcrew House, resurrected as an eyecatcher, 1994.
HECTOR MCDONNELL

Oliver Plunkett's Church. (53.731688,-7.1395436) There are grand herbaceous borders, a beautiful 17th century gate and viewing mound plus an avenue of ancient yews and a fairy trail for children. You can take lunch or tea in the sunny teahouse there. WEBSITE: *loughcrew.com*

The hills between Kells and Oldcastle are dotted with the mounds of other passage graves. Part of one survives as the superb standing stone on the hill called **Kingsmountain**,(537617-704078). It is quite hard to find. From Loughcrew, take

17th century gateway in Loughcrew Historic Gardens.
PHOTO: ROBERT O'BYRNE

93

Neolithic standing stone at Kingsmountain.
HECTOR MCDONNELL

the road south for **Ballinlough** and turn left in the village. Drive to what appears to be a crossroads, keep to the right and take the next left turn. There should be a bungalow on your left; walk up the grassy lane to the right of it and you will come to a bend with the stone in the field just ahead. The far side of the stone is covered with delicately carved spirals. Originally it formed the lintel of a passage grave stuffed with bones which a farmer flattened out in the late 19th century. Many other prehistoric graves have probably gone the same way. In 1849, William Wilde reported that burial mounds on the hill of Tara were still being used by farmers as a source of gravel.

By 600 AD, the area around Loughcrew had become an important monastic centre with several churches. There was one at **Clonabreany** just north of Crossakiel where St Oliver Plunkett's parents are buried. There are six slabs just inside the gate of the graveyard dating from the 9th century inscribed with crosses and inscriptions. Even before that, Clonabreany was probably a pagan burial site, there are two standing stones in the northwest corner of the graveyard. Don't miss further up the same road towards Crossakiel, the tiny model village of **Ardglasson** (53.711951,-7.039355) two picturesque terraces of labourers' cottages facing each other. They were probably built in the early 19th century for workers on the Battersby estate. Some are now let as holiday houses or writers' retreats (Maeve Binchy is said to have worked there) and have had some alterations but they still retains their unity and charm.

At Crossakiel on the top of the hill, take the road southeast to **Kilskyre.** This was once the site of **St Schiama's Church.** Schiama was the great granddaughter

94

19th century model village at Ardglasson. PHOTO: THOMAS PAKENHAM

of Niall of the Nine Hostages, (High King when St Patrick was brought to Ireland as a slave) and was famous for her penances and love of fasting. The settlement was plundered by Danes in 949 AD and later by the Normans before being awarded to the Nugent family. A small lane opposite the modern Catholic church leads to the earlier graveyard with ancient gravestones and a small ruined **Nugent mausoleum**.

Take the road southwest again to **Clonmellon**. This model village was laid out by the Chapman family in the late 18th century with a specially wide street designed for cattle fairs. The family also built a grand classical house here, **Killua Castle,** (53.6596064,-6.9982728) just west of the town. It was gothicised by the architect James

Gravestone with Nugent coat-of-arms.
HECTOR MCDONNELL

95

Gothick gatelodge for Killua Castle, designed by James Sheil, 1820s.
HECTOR MCDONNELL

Sheil in 1830 who added assorted towers and a large wing. In the 1890s, the 7th baronet, Sir Thomas Chapman, caused scandal by eloping with his daughters' governess, a Miss Lawrence. They had 4 brilliant sons, one of them becoming the famous Lawrence of Arabia. They might have inherited the house if Lady Chapman had agreed to give her husband a divorce. The house was eventually sold to dismantlers after the Second World War and became a ruin. In 2004 it was bought by an Austrian banker, and he and his wife have restored it superbly and made a deer park around the house.

Accessible by appointment. WEBSITE: *killuacastle.com*

Killua had fascinating assorted gate lodges of which three survive, two gothic and one classical. Take the right fork at the northern end of the village (right of the N52) and follow the roads around the estate, turning left. The first lodge you come to is a miniature castle, recently restored, and just past it is a footpath leading to the so-called **Potato Monument**, an obelisk commemorating Sir Walter Raleigh's first planting of the potato in Ireland. It was erected in 1810, 35

Monument to Sir Walter Raleigh, to celebrate his planting of the potato.
The now restored castle of Killua can be seen behind.
HECTOR MCDONNELL

years before the potato blight struck, plunging Ireland into the Great Famine.

Grove Gardens (53.6681875,-6.912949) Fordstown, east of Clonmellon, signposted off RI64. A pretty 4 acre garden planted with a huge variety of clematis and roses. Adjoining it are purpose built aviaries filled with exotic birds, and there is a small pet farm for children. You can bring a picnic to eat on seating provided and there is usually tea or coffee available.

WEBSITE: *ireland-guide.com/gardens/grove-gardens-.7091.html*

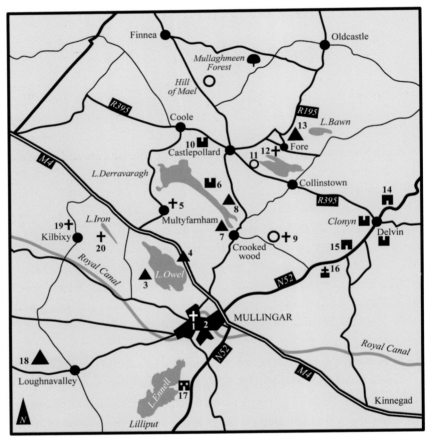

Castle	1 *Christ the King Cathedral*	11 *Turgesius's Fort*
Hill	2 *Greville Arms Hotel*	12 *St Fechin's Church, Fore Abbey*
Forest	3 *Slanemore Hill*	13 *Ben of Fore*
Church	4 *Captain's Hill*	14 *The Rosmead Gate*
Fort	5 *Multyfarnham Franciscan Abbey*	15 *Bracklyn Gate House*
Entrance	6 *Mortimer's Castle*	16 *The Beehive Tomb*
House	7 *Knock Ross*	17 *Belvedere House and Gardens*
Tomb	8 *Knock Eyon*	18 *The Hill of Uisneach*
	9 *St Munna's Church*	19 *St Bigseach's Church*
	10 *Tullynally Castle and Gardens*	20 *Tristenagh Abbey*

In and around mullingar

Mullingar (53.524348,-7.3424142) The name comes from the Irish An Muileann gCaer meaning the Left handed Mill. The town was founded by the Norman knight, William Petit in 1186 and became the county town when Western Meath was divided from Meath in 1545. The land around was famous for fattening cattle and "Beef to the Heels like a Mullingar heifer" remains a well known insult (or compliment) to this day.

The town flourished after the **Royal Canal** reached it in 1806; it circles the town on three sides and the footpaths make agreeable walks. There are now also two impressive new **Greenways** or bicycle tracks, one towards Longford alongside the canal, the other following the old railway track to Athlone.

The town itself has a handsome early 19th century market house, now the tourist office, and theatre (now the Arts centre) and an immense **Cathedral** dedicated to **Christ the King**. Designed by Ralph Byrne, it was begun in

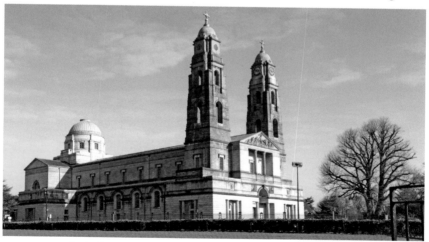

Cathedral of Christ the King, Mullingar, completed in 1939.
PHOTO BY THOMAS PAKENHAM

Boris Anrep's mosaic of St Patrick lighting his Paschal fire at Slane, in the Cathedral of Christ the King. PHOTO BY THOMAS PAKENHAM the 1920s and officially opened the day before the Second World War broke out. Its twin towers and dome can be spotted from miles away. Inside, the transept has **mosaic murals** by the Russian painter, Boris Anrep, who also designed the mosaic floors of London's Tate Gallery. The mosaic to the right depicts St Patrick lighting his Pascal fire on the Hill of Slane and blasting a pagan idol into three pieces while a snake slithers away in one corner.

Mullingar's oldest hotel, the **Greville Arms** (halfway down the high street) has a fascinating small museum with relics from the surrounding lakes, including a Neolithic stone axe, and an ammonite dating from 150,000 BC.

Lough Owel (53.5754694,-7.3684656) 2km west off Mullingar is a beautiful Blue Flag lake whose water supplies the town and the Royal Canal. To the west of the lake is **Slanemore Hill** which is mentioned in the great 8th century Irish epic, the Táin (known in English as The Cattle Raid of Cooley). It has three well marked Bronze Age barrows on its summit.

The lake itself is excellent for swimming; there is an official bathing place signposted along its eastern shore with a diving board and stone jetty. You can swim out to a wooded island, in your depth almost all the way. It was to one of the islands here that a notorious Danish warlord Turgesius was lured in the 9th century by the Uí Néill king, Malachy I. Turgesius wanted to marry the King's daughter and the cunning king proposed that he should meet her and her handmaidens there. But no sooner had Turgesius dismissed his followers than the handmaidens revealed themselves as muscular young warriors who seized him and bound him in chains. King Malachy had him rolled down **Captain's Hill** (east of the lake) in a barrel studded with nails and then drowned. The gruesome tale was told with relish three hundred years later by the Norman historian, Gerald of Wales. Turgesius is said to have had his main stronghold beside Lough Lene, and is said to have collected an annual tribute of an ounce of gold from every family in his power.

Multyfarnham (53.6284922,-7.3941619), set in the hills to the north of Lough Owel is one of Westmeath's prettiest villages, with a prize-winning pub serving lunches and dinners in the main street. The 15th century **Franciscan Abbey** is still used as the local Catholic church. Until recently,

Ruins of Multyfarnham Abbey. ENGRAVED AFTER GEORGE PETRIE,
T.K. CROMWELL'S *EXCURSIONS THROUGH IRELAND,* 1821

the monks ran an agricultural college next door and there is an eccentric
Stations of the Cross in the garden outside their monastery with statuary
modelled on local parishioners. A road from here leads to the western shore
of **Lough Derravaragh**, where there is a caravan park of the site of an old
country house, and you can usually hire a boat.

Lough Derravaragh, just north of Multyfarnham, is famous for its
association with the legend of the Children of Lir. They were pushed into
the lake by their jealous stepmother and turned to swans but allowed to
keep their human voices. Their father, King Lir would come to sit by the
lake to hear them singing. The legend may have some basis in fact. There is
an ancient crannog at the other end of the lake (on the Coolure shore) with
a causeway to a large ringfort which is thought to have been the stronghold
of some local king. Excavated in the 1990s, both crannog and ringfort have
yielded much treasure, gold torcs, brooches, even a scales for weighing gold
and silver. Maybe this was King Lir's castle?

Swans on Lough Derravaragh, home of the legendary Children of Lir.
HECTOR MCDONNELL

The lake has numerous other crannogs, though none so early and there are the remains of a fortress known as **Mortimer's Castle** halfway along the eastern shore.(The Earl of Mortimer was a powerful Norman lord who at one point became *de facto* ruler of England and Ireland). The southern end is guarded by two wooded hills, **Knock Ross** and **Knock Eyon**; in medieval times , a hermit lived by a holy well half way down Knock Eyon.(53.6300519,-7.3050848). You can still climb the path to it (start from the back of the hill by Streamstown 2km north of **Crooked Wood**). Sir Henry Piers in his 17th century history of Westmeath describes how Catholic pilgrims would make their way to drink from the well to purge their sins, "then having paid off the old score...they return to a certain green spot of ground...and fall to dancing and carousing the rest of the day...as if they celebrated the Bacchanalia, rather than the memory of a Pious saint." Both hills still have the remains of the ancient oak woods from which Derravaragh ("Lake of the oaks") takes its name. Crooked Wood commemorates the crooked oaks once valuable for shipbuilding.

St Munna's Church, Taghmon (53.6009674,-7.2707829), 1km southeast of Crooked Wood, is a well preserved 15th century church with vaulted stone roof. It has a fortified four-storey tower to which the priest could retire for safety. One priest was said to be so lazy that he would only descend from his tower when the congregation had put sufficient money in a basket which he

15th century church of St Munna's, Taghmon with fortified tower. A sheela-na-gig is inset above the window right of the door. HECTOR MCDONNELL

lowered to them. The church has a carved head over the door and a **sheela-na-gig** above a window on the north wall. (In Ireland, the name sheela-na-gig was said to be that of St Patrick's wife who would help women bear the pains of childbirth – but the name in fact is a corruption of St Cecilia and sheela-na-gigs are found in medieval churches all over Britain and Europe.)

Originally there was a large monastery here and you can still see some of its stone walls across the road. It was sacked by the McGeoghegans in 1457. And on the hill above, (now private farmland) look for the **Norman motte** which once surveyed the whole length of Lough Derravaragh and the surrounding countryside.

Castlepollard (53.6800841,-7.3052056) at the western end of Lough Derravaragh, takes its name from the Pollards who settled here in Elizabethan times. It has two different names in Irish: one is Baile Na Gross, meaning Town of the Crosses or crossroads – the other Cion Torc, meaning Hill of the Boar. The hill is said to be where Diarmuid was gored by a wild boar and bled to death. According to the famous legend, Gráinne, who was with him, begged Finn McCool to bring him water as he lay dying but the jealous Finn let the water spill through his hands.

The town was laid out by the Pollards in the early 1800s around a green with a handsome market house (now awaiting restoration) and parish church at one end, and plenty of space for cattlefairs. The Pollards left for Scotland in the 1920s and their house, bought by nuns, is now sadly empty.

Tullynally Castle (53.683532,-7.32941) 2km to the west (R394)is the home of the town's rival landlords, the Pakenhams, who arrived here in the 17th century. Henry Pakenham built himself a large semi fortified house overlooking Lough Derravaragh. In 1740, his grandson, Thomas Pakenham married an heiress from Co. Longford and acquired her large estates and family title. In 1800, his grandson, the 2nd Earl of Longford had the house remodelled by Francis Johnston as a Gothic Revival castle, and then 20 years later by his pupil, James Sheil. (*see p.25*) In the 1840s, the architect Sir Richard Morrison doubled its size with two enormous wings, mostly designed as servants' quarters. It is now probably the largest castle in Ireland still surviving as a family home.

The surrounding **parkland** is open for walkers all year round; and the gardens throughout the summer. (Check times on the website.) There are **walled flower gardens** (one is now also home to a family of llamas), and 10 hectares of romantic **woodland gardens** set around two ornamental

ABOVE: *Tullynally castle (formerly Pakenham Hall) viewed from the south, with the Hill of Mael behind.*
BELOW: *Chinese pagoda and waterfall in the woodland gardens at Tullynally.*
PHOTOS: THOMAS PAKENHAM

106

lakes. The current owner, Thomas Pakenham has a passion for trees and has collected plants from all over the world – look for rare magnolias and maples, primulas and woodland lilies. There are pretty summerhouses and an **18th century grotto** at the top of the gardens where you can glimpse Lough Derravaragh through the trees.

The castle courtyard has a sunny tearoom where you can eat indoors or out. Tours of the castle itself are usually available by appointment. WEBSITE: *tullynallycastle.ie*

Lough Lene (53.6615856,-7.2021289), 3.2km east of Castlepollard, is another Blue Flag lake where the locals like to swim. If you turn first left off the road to Delvin, you can drive along its eastern shore and see the humps of long cyst graves known as **Gallagher's Moteens** on the green hills to the left. A little further along a track on the right leads to Castlepollard's reservoir, and an enormous hill fort, Rindoon, also known as **Turgesius's Fort**. Turgesius was the Danish warlord who once ruled in Dublin and threatened the power of the southern Uí Néill. In 845 AD, he offered to marry the Uí Néill king's daughter, and was lured to an island in Lough Owel to be captured and drowned *(see Lough Owel)* But the ringfort itself pre-dates Turgesius and may go back to Bronze Age times: there a straight line running from it via the long cyst graves on the far side of Lough Lene to the cairns on the Loughcrew hills.

Accessible by permission.

Fore (53.6623105,-7.2446932), 6km north of Castlepollard (R195) is one of the jewels of Westmeath. Set in a beautiful secluded valley, it is now a tiny one-horse village but was once a walled Norman town. You can still see the two town gates south and north of the village.

Fore was founded by St Fechin in 630 AD. He was a powerful saint, much respected by the Normans. (Gerald of Wales tells the story of one of Hugh de Lacy's men being consumed by fire after desecrating his shrine). **St Fechin's Church** is just south of the village, built into the side of a steep hill. It has a massive lintel stone which the saint is said to have wafted into the air after the workmen were unable to lift it – one of the **Seven Wonders** or miracles

Doorway and lintel stone of St Fechin's church.
DRAWN BY GEORGE PETRIE

of Fore. The chancel was added in the early 13th century; don't miss the carved figure of a seated monk with bulging eyes supporting one side of the chancel arch.

There are six other miracles associated with Fore: the Abbey built in a quaking bog, the Mill without a race, the Tree which won't burn, the Water which flows up hill, the Well whose water will not boil, and the Anchorite in a stone. The water that flows uphill comes through a limestone fissure from Lough Lene nearby, and the **Anchorite in a stone** was Patrick Beglin who walled himself up in a tower just above St Fechin's Church, and was fed through an arrowslit by his neighbours. He was Ireland's last hermit and died in 1616. (The tower was restored by the Greville Nugent family in the 19th century who added a vaulted mausoleum.) The unfortunate tree that won't burn, now covered with rags, and the well whose water won't boil can be seen on the new path from the car park across the "quaking bog" to the **Benedictine Abbey**.

Panoramic view of Fore. From right to left, St Fechin's church, the Benedictine Abbey, the Anchorite's tower and the Nugent mausoleum. HECTOR MCDONNELL

108

Ruins of the 14th century Benedectine Abbey; note the defensive towers.
PHOTO: THOMAS PAKENHAM

The 14th century abbey is quite substantial; at its peak, it had over 300 monks here and there is a charming central cloister, with lilies carved on the pillars. But it soon found itself "beyond the Pale" and was under constant attack by "Irish rebels". There are two tall defensive towers with arrowslits and a stone in the cloister is said to be where the monks sharpened their swords. The last Prior, William Nugent, surrendered peacefully to Henry VIII in 1539 who granted him a pension for the rest of his days. You can take a looped walk from the Abbey's gatehouse across the road and up the hill opposite, known as the **Ben of Fore**, and then descend by the Catholic church at the north of the village. Or climb to the top of the hill from which (on a clear day) you can see 11 lakes.

To find the prettiest of all the Westmeath lakes, continue past the Catholic church towards Dromone (R195) and you will come to **Lough Bawn** on your left. Bawn means white and the bottom of the lake is made of white marl, making it very clear but treacherous for swimming. The boundary between Westmeath and modern Meath is said to lie in at the lake's centre.

Finnea (53.781128,-7.390447) 10km north of Castlepollard (R194). This is where the Inny river crosses the border into Cavan. The bridge over it was famously defended by **Miles the Slasher** against General Monro's army in 1646 during the Confederate Wars. There is a memorial to him at the top of the main street.

Delvin castle, built by Hugh de Lacy, half destroyed by Cromwell. HECTOR MCDONNELL

3km away to the southeast is the **Forest of Mullaghmeen** (53.7489671,-7.3001874), planted in the 1930s and now the largest beech forest in Ireland, covering over a thousand acres. There is a network of paths and an ancient rath at the centre. The wood is full of flowering bluebells and anemones in late spring. To the south is the **Hill of Mael**, with a spectacular rock face on one side known as the **Rock of Corry.** The ring fort on top is said to have been a stronghold of the once powerful king of Breffney, Tiernan O'Rourke, who was killed when he came to parley with Hugh de Lacy on the Hill of Down.

Delvin (35.6111464,-7.0959813) to the northeast was once an important outpost of the Pale. The first castle was built here by Hugh de Lacy in 1181 for his son in law Gilbert de Nugent, who was granted lordship of the surrounding territory. It was partly destroyed by Cromwell in 1657 and only the east and west towers remain. Another, **Clonyn** was built in the 1870s by his descendant, daughter of the last Earl of Westmeath. You can see its gates just outside the town. It is still privately owned and not usually accessible but makes a splendid silhouette from the hills to the north of the town.

Clonyn Castle, built 1870 by the last Earl of Westmeath. HECTOR MCDONNELL

Delvin is also famous – or notorious – as the inspiration for Brinsley MacNamara's novel, *The Valley of the Squinting Windows*, about lives ruined by malicious gossip. When the book was first published in 1918, outraged locals had it publicly burned and Brinsley MacNamara's father, the local schoolmaster, was boycotted. He fought and won a high court case against those who claimed to have been libelled in the novel. The novel is still in print.

The Rosmead Gate (53.6265984,-7.0728865) 3km east of Delvin on N52. Pause to admire all that remains of one of the grandest gates in Ireland. The original gateway was commissioned in 1803 by Robert Smyth of Glananea House outside Drumcree and was three times the size with statues in niches at either side and a stone unicorn on top. There were several landowners called Smyth in Westmeath, and soon he was known as Smyth of the Gate. His grandson became fed up with the title and sold the gate in the 1860s, but to his chagrin then became known as "Smyth without the Gate." The unicorn and niches

The Rosmead gate – all that remains.
HECTOR MCDONNELL

111

The fantastic gatelodge to Bracklyn House. HECTOR MCDONNELL

with their statues have long disappeared but a few pieces of the original Coade stone ornament still remain on the elegant limestone arch, now the gateway to Lord Rosmead's distant roofless house.

Bracklyn Gate House (53.5691198,-7.1077332), signposted just south of Delvin on the N52, is probably the most fantastical gate lodge in Ireland. A plaque over the central arch dates it to 1821, and it was probably designed by Francis Johnston the year before his death for Bracklyn's landowner, James Fetherston-Haugh. Made of eroded limestone boulders, it has a room each side of the arch with bellcast slated roofs and has recently been beautifully restored by the current owner. The main house at Bracklyn (not accessible) built 30 years earlier is by contrast a plain classical house. But the Fetherston-Haughs must have enjoyed fantasy as there is mausoleum of elaborate eroded rockwork behind the house.

The Beehive Tomb, Reynella. This extraordinary monument (recently restored) can be found in the graveyard of St John's Parish Church. It was built in 1835 by Adolphus Cooke, a highly eccentric landowner who believed his father, Robert Cooke would be re-incarnated as a bee. Adolphus was illegitimate, born to a servant girl and was brought up in a thatched cottage by a nurse and forbidden to speak to his father. But his two legitimate half brothers died young and he unexpectedly inherited the substantial Cookesborough estate. He believed he himself would be re-incarnated as a fox and changed his will in old age to disinherit a cousin who he discovered had recently killed a fox out hunting. He built himself a large marble vault complete with fireplace, marble chair and table where he himself planned to be interred, but after his death in 1876, the local clergyman refused to bury him there and instead he was interred in the beehive tomb with his father and his old nurse, Mary Kelly.

Lough Ennell (53.4475958,-7.4383984) Mullingar's favourite lake and playground. (*See also Belvedere.*) **Lilliput** on the southwest shore, takes its name from the tiny race of people in Swift's *Gulliver's Travels*. **Swift** used to stay here with the Rochfort family. (*See Belvedere.*) There is a small ruined house set back from the shore and facing it a tiny island with a statue on it of the Goddess of Plenty, known as the White Lady. To the left is **Cro-Inish island**, for 300 years the lake dwelling of the Uí Néill High Kings of Ireland. Their main stronghold was 3.2km north, the large mound known as **Dún na Sciath** – Fort of the Shields. From here they controlled the road from Tara to the royal burial ground at **Clonmacnoise** and exacted tribute from as far away as Viking Dublin. Several gold ornaments have been found here (now in the National Museum in Dublin) and King Malachy's "lost collar of gold" is still believed be buried in the lake.

Belvedere House and Gardens (53.4772002,-7.3713907), 6km west of Mullingar on N52. A classical villa on the shores of Lough Ennell designed in 1740 by Richard Castle for Robert Rochfort, 1st Earl of Belvedere. It was originally planned as a grand fishing lodge, but the "wicked earl" as he became known, moved there full time after locking up his young wife Mary Molesworth in his earlier house at Gaulstown after she had confessed (under duress) to adultery with his brother Arthur. She was imprisoned there for 33 years until his death. Arthur was sued for *crim.con.* (criminal conversation) and made bankrupt and died in jail. Lord Belvedere later quarrelled with another brother and commissioned one of Ireland's most spectacular follies, known as the **Jealous Wall** to blot out the view of his house at Tudenham, a mile away along the lake shore.

The villa itself has fine rococo plasterwork – look for Jupiter hurling thunderbolts in the front hall and sleeping cupids in a starry moonlit sky

The Jealous Wall at Belvedere, said to have been built by Lord Belvedere to block out the view of his brother's grander house. HECTOR MCDONNELL

in the adjoining dining room. Walks through Belevedere's demesne lead to two early 18th century follies, a **gothick gazebo** (said to have been inspired by the monks' lavabo at Mellifont) and a fantastic **rustic archway** of eroded stones. Both are said to have come from designs by Thomas Wright of Durham, who had been working in nearby Louth. Terraces with heavy balustrades below the house were added in the late 19th century, rather spoiling the romantic view of the lake.

In 1912, the house was inherited by Colonel Charles Howard Bury, leader of the first reconnaissance of Mount Everest in 1921. He later brought back seeds of rare plants and trees from the Himalayas to stock the walled gardens. After his death, the house, gardens and demesne were bought by Westmeath Co. Council who roofed over the courtyard behind the Jealous wall to create a visitor centre and café.

Accessible all year. WEBSITE: *belvedere-house.ie*

The Hill of Uisneach (53.4838823,-7.5582773), 10km southwest of Mullingar. One of the most important Iron Age sites in Ireland, it is said to mark Ireland's mystical centre or navel of Ireland and was the original meeting

114

The Catstone or Stone of the Divisions, said to be the mystic centre of Ireland.
HECTOR MCDONNELL

place for its tribal leaders and kings. An enormous glacial boulder known as the **Catstone** or **Stone of the Divisions** is said to marks the place that four Fir Bolg brothers divided up Ireland between them and then allotted a portion each to their youngest brother, Slaine (*see the Hill of Slane*) creating the 5th province of Meath or Midhe. Under the Stone, the earth goddess Eriu from whom Ireland takes its name is said to be buried and at the summit, another stone marks **St Patrick's Bed**. He is supposed to have called here in the 5th century. Another legend (quoted by Geoffrey of Monmouth in his Historia Regum Britanniae) claims that it was from the Hill of Uisneach that the wizard Merlin transposed by magic the stones of Stonehenge to their present place in England!

Like Tara, Uisneach needs imagination and luckily there is usually a local guide or storyteller on hand to help. There are fine views but otherwise few visible remains: excavations have found a few souterrains and remains of Iron Age houses. There are also traces of the ancient ritual bonfires, and a festival of fire or Bealtaine is now held here almost every summer.
Accessible in summer by appointment. WEBSITE: *uisneach.ie*

St Brigid's Well, Killare. HECTOR MCDONNELL

St Brigid's Well (53.535385-6.594004) is only 500m to the west of Uisneach, (just off R390). Brigid was originally a pagan fertility goddess, later transformed into a Christian saint, and her wells are found all over Ireland. Stop at the Uisneach Inn and walk up the slope just behind it. The well is now a pretty teardrop shaped pool with a stone shrine to the saint added at one end.

Kilbixy, St Bigseach's Church (53.6031912,-7.5157832) lies 3km north of Ballynacargy village in the old Baronstown demesne. Nearly hidden by trees, this elegant little Parish church was probably designed by the famous English architect, James Wyatt for Lord Sunderlin whose mausoleum stands beside it. (Lord Sunderlin had a huge Palladian house nearby, now no longer existent.) In 1962, half the church roof fell in, luckily when the church was empty, and only part of it was rebuilt. Inside are an early Christian cross and a medieval font, both probably from an earlier church on the site. The church is locked except when used for services.

Kilbixy was once an important Norman settlement; you can see the original Norman motte north of the church and the walls of a tower house to the southeast, but it was plundered and burnt by the O'Neills in 1430. In the 18th century, labourers discovered an extraordinary network of souterrains nearby. The Malone section of the graveyard has an impressive array of late 19th century Celtic crosses, each with a tiny stone chapel on its top. The whole place has been beautifully restored.

St Bigseach's church and Lord Sunderlin's mausoleum.
PHOTO: THOMAS PAKENHAM

Only a mile to the east, beside Lough Iron are the overgrown ruins of **Tristenagh Abbey**, once an Augustinian priory and leper hospital. It was closed and plundered after the Dissolution, but its new owner, Henry Piers became a Catholic convert and partly restored it. His son, Sir Henry Piers was the first historian of Westmeath. The abbey was abandoned in 1807 when his great grandson, Sir John Piers, seduced his friend's wife, Lady Cloncurry for a bet, was sued for *crim. con.* (criminal conversation) and had to flee to the Isle of Man. John Betjeman wrote a poem about him "The Ballad of Sir John Piers".

More accessible than the Abbey itself is the ruined 15th century church, **Temple Cross** at the entrance to its demesne. Inside is a worn monument to the first Henry Piers with his armorial crest, framed by angels and you can climb the narrow staircase up the tower to the little chamber where the resident priest once lived.

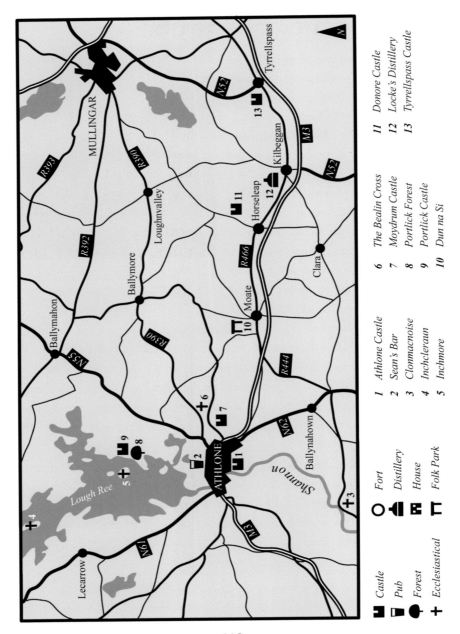

1 Athlone Castle   6 The Bealin Cross   11 Donore Castle
2 Sean's Bar   7 Moydrum Castle   12 Locke's Distillery
3 Clonmacnoise   8 Portlick Forest   13 Tyrrellspass Castle
4 Inchcleraun   9 Portlick Castle
5 Inchmore   10 Dun na Si

Castle
Pub
Forest
Ecclesiastical

Fort
Distillery
House
Folk Park

in and around athlone

Athlone (53.4230832,-7.9449051) lies on the extreme western border on the old Kingdom of Meath, and straddles the Shannon with half the town in Connaught. It has been an important crossing point for at least 5,000 years and was heavily fortified throughout the middle ages.

Athlone Castle was built in 1210 by John de Grey, Justiciar of Norman Ireland and later became the headquarters for the Lord President of Connaught. It now has a series of galleries depicting local history from Viking times until the present. In 1690, after King James II's defeat at the Battle of the Boyne, Athlone became a crucial battleground for the Jacobite and

The North gate, Athlone, early 1800s. Erected circa 1570 to reinforce Athlone's defences, it was demolished in the early 20th century. Northgate street marks the line of the old town walls. DANIEL GROSE

Sean's bar, Athlone, the oldest pub in Ireland. HECTOR MCDONNELL

Williamite armies, facing each other across the Shannon. After two prolonged sieges, the Williamite General, de Ginkel, managed to find a crossing further south and attack the Jacobite army on their flank, forcing them to flee further west and south. A circular room in the castle's Upper Keep brilliantly recreates the **Siege Experience** using the latest sight and sound technology.
WEBSITE: *athlonecastle.ie*

120

and 5 star meal on board with Romaris Cruises. (WEBSITE: *athlone.ie/visit/ romaris-cruise-boat/*)

Lough Ree – the Lake of the Kings – is the third largest lake in Ireland and even appears on Ptolemy's map of the known world in the 2nd century AD. Part of the Shannon system, it has borders on 3 counties, Westmeath, Longford and Roscommon and marks the furthest extent of the old kingdom of Meath to the west. It is studded with islands and hidden reefs – boats should take care to follow the channels marked. Many of the islands were once home to religious orders. **Inchcleraun** has seven churches. The largest island, **Inchmore**, had a 12th century Augustinian priory which survived till Henry VIII's Dissolution. (*See also Saints Island and Rathcline Castle in Co. Longford*). You can take a cruise around the lake from Athlone or hire a boat to visit the islands yourself. Ask the visitor centre in Athlone for details.

There are some good restaurants on inlets from the lake, notably at Glasson, just north of Athlone, such as Grogan's, Wineport Lodge or the Villager Bar.

The Bealin Cross (53.4351522,-7.8471077) stands on a small hillock in Twyford demesne, 6km northeast of Athlone. Take the unnamed road south from R390 and there is a stile and path leading to the cross. Originally the cross was found at Bealin a mile away, hence its name, but it may have been brought from Clonmacnoise by an abbot named Tuathgall who lived in these parts around 810 AD. An inscription on the west face reads "Pray for Tuathgall who caused this cross to be made". The east face has a lion at the

The 9th century Bealin Cross.
HECTOR MCDONNELL

Moydrum Castle in its prime. FROM J.P. NEALE'S *VIEWS OF SEATS*, 1823

bottom and there is a scroll of interlaced creatures with bird like heads running up the shaft. The west face has three panels, one of a hunter armed with a spear, above him a stag at bay with a hound biting its leg.

Moydrum Castle (53.4280695,-7.8654522) 9.6km east of Athlone – a theatrical Jacobean castle designed by Sir Richard Morrison in 1814 for the first baron Castlemaine, then the largest landowner in Westmeath. It was burnt by the IRA in 1921 and is now a spectacular ivy-clad ruin. It was made famous as the cover of' U2's *Unforgettable Fire* album in 1984. The ruin is on private land but you can admire it from the road.

Portlick Forest (53.4915508,-7.9191072) A wonderful 5km walk around the Whinning peninsula projecting out into Lough Ree. You can either approach it by boat, anchoring in Portlick bay (watch out for rocks just below the surface) or take the N55 to Glasson or Toberclare. There is a car park on the north shore of Rinardoo Bay. Much of the walk is through deciduous woodland or along the shores of Lough Ree. One large glade contains the stump of a tower house. And you can also catch a glimpse of

Portlick Castle (now privately owned). This was built by the Dillon family who came to Ireland with King John and were granted large estates east of Lough Ree. They lived there till 1690 until forced to flee to France after the Williamite Wars. The castle was sold by the crown to one of the Westmeath family of Smyths (*see p.111, Rosmead Gate*) who added a Georgian wing and then gothicised it in 1860 to match the original castle. It was burned down soon after and fell into ruin. An enterprising Australian bought it in 1988 and fully restored it.

Dún na Sí, Lake Road, Moate. (53.4002096,-7.7398253) Set up by local enterprise, this is a folk park with a whole lot of things packed in. Part of it is an amenity park for families, set around a **turlough** or small limestone lake which disappears mysteriously at times in summer. The lake is a haven for birds, including swans which you can view discreetly from a hide without disturbing them.

Adjoining it is an imaginative **heritage park**, designed to let you explore local history through time. There are recreations of a Neolithic cromlech, a stone circle and ring fort, a hedge school (where Catholics were taught during the time of the penal laws) a thatched fisherman's cottage, an early 19th century stone farmhouse and a blacksmith's forge (often complete with blacksmith) and a small pet farm. Next door is a small **rural museum** with a collection of traditional farm tools. To complete the experience, there is an excellent café serving coffee and snacks. WEBSITE: *visitwestmeath.ie*

Next door is Westmeath's **Genealogical Centre**, where you can get help to trace an ancestor or undertake local historical research. It is best to book well in advance. WEBSITE: *dunnasi.ie*

Horse Leap Village (53.392336,-7.581356) on the Offaly/Westmeath border is said to take its name from the famous leap made by Hugh de Lacy across the moat of his castle when fleeing from the McGeoghegans soon after he had been appointed the new Lord of Meath. The leap is commemorated by a bronze statue of a leaping horse on the village green. De Lacy's castle Ardmulchan no longer exists but Brian McGeoghegan, married to the King of Offaly's daughter, built himself a fine tower house, **Donore Castle**, in 1598 which still stands in the

fields nearby. Look for his plaque on its south face and the carved head of a king and a bishop above the entrance arch. It was restored in 1809 by Richard Nagle, Brian McGeoghegan's descendant, and inhabited until the 1950s.
Accessible by permission.

Locke's Distillery, Kilbeggan (53.3692984,-7.5050084) is said to be Ireland's oldest surviving whiskey distillery, established in 1757. It still has its original 18th and 19th century machinery, including an early steam engine and massive waterwheel. Present owners have restored it as a major tourist attraction and there is an excellent café serving among other things delicious whiskey-flavoured cakes.
WEBSITE: *kilbegganwhiskey.com*

Tyrellspass (53.385963,-7.3838104) takes its name from the Norman Tyrells who once controlled much of the surrounding plains. There is an effigy said to be of Sir John Tyrell in the ruined church northwest of Rochfortbridge. In 1597, his son, Richard Tyrell routed an English army here, killing a thousand men. The Tyrells' 15th century **tower house** has now been converted to a restaurant and small museum.
WEBSITE: *tyrellspasscastle.com*

Locke's distillery, Kilbeggan – Ireland's oldest surviving whiskey distillery.
HECTOR MCDONNELL

Tyrellspass Castle, now a restaurant and small museum. HECTOR MCDONNELL

Don't miss the charming crescent of houses around a **village green** just east of the castle. It was commissioned by Jane, Countess of Belvedere in the 1830s. She and her two husbands have memorials in the adjoining church.

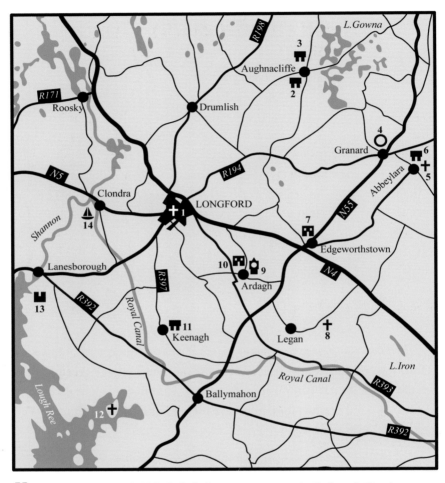

■	Castle	1	St Mels Cathedral
⛫	Megalitic site	2	Aughnacliff Dolmen
⚲	Clock Tower	3	Grania's Bed
✝	Church	4	Norman Motte and Village
○	Fort	5	Cistercian Abbey
⚓	Harbour	6	The Cartronbore Stone Circle
⌂	House	7	Maria Edgeworth Centre

8	Rathreagh Church
9	Gothick Clocktower
10	Ardagh House
11	The Corlea Trackway
12	Augustinian priory
13	Rathcline Castle
14	Richmond Harbour

130

in and around longford

Longford is one of the few large towns not founded by Vikings or Normans. The first settlement was by the powerful O'Farrell clan after their old stronghold at Granard had been destroyed by Edward Bruce in the early 14th century. The river Camlin gives it access to the Shannon, 10km away.

Its star attraction is **St Mel's Cathedral** (53.7269563,-7.7984037) to the east of the town. Begun in 1840, this huge building has been described as a prayer in stone, built with the pennies of the faithful over 60 years. The original architect was John Benjamin Keane, who had already helped to build the Catholic Pro-Cathedral in Dublin. Money ran out during the Famine years and the campanile tower was erected 20 years later. Finally in the 1890s, George Ashlin added the entrance portico: its entablature, sculpted by George

Interior of St Mel's cathedral, reconstructed following the fire.

Smith, shows St Mel enthroned as first bishop of Ardagh and Clonmacnoise.

The rather plain exterior does not prepare you for the magnificent neoclassical interior with double rows of freestanding Ionic columns crowned by angels. The cathedral was burnt down accidentally on Christmas Day 2009, but has been beautifully restored, including the original stained glass windows (in the transept) made by Harry Clarke. There are new stained windows by James Scanlon and Stations of the Cross sculpted by Ken Thompson. It was re-opened for church services exactly 5 years after it was burnt. Website: *longford.ie/en/visit/explore-the-past/st-mel-s-cathedral/st-mel-s-cathedral.html*

Aughnacliff (53.8478695,-7.6090069), 22km northeast of Longford, beside Lough Gowna, has one of the most unusual dolmens or portal tombs in Ireland. To find it, take the lane through a wooden gate 100m past Aughnacliff Church, and cross the field to the further side. The dolmen is just below you. It has two capstones balanced precariously on each other; the upper capstone is huge, 3m by 1.5m. One investigator has described it as looking like a giant stone poodle! It dates to around 3,000 BC.

Portal tomb at Aughnacliff, with two capstones. HECTOR MCDONNELL

The portal tomb at Cleenrath known as Grania's Bed. HECTOR MCDONNELL

There is another much smaller portal tomb known as "**Grania's Bed**" at **Cleenrath** nearby, just north of Aughnacliff. Take the first right for Gowna and next left up a small track. The tomb is about 300m up this track on the field to the right. The name commemorates the famous legend of Gráinne's flight across Ireland with her lover Diarmuid, pursued by her would-be husband Finn McCool. They slept in a lot of places! (*See also Cion Torc hill outside Castlepollard for the story of Diarmuid's death.*)

Granard (53.7751897,-7.5013702) A town that boasts the tallest motte in Ireland, built by Richard de Tuite in 1199 when he was granted the surrounding territory by Hugh de Lacy. The bawn below it is now being developed as a **Living History Village** featuring a replica Viking longship, a forge, a bakery, a jousting area and a banqueting hall, but you can already visit the existing Norman exhibition open daily.

WEBSITE: *www.knightsandconquests.ie*

The site was an important stronghold long before the Vikings or Normans arrived. The old boundary between Ulster and the rest of Ireland, the Black Pig's Dyke, lies alongside the town. There was a famous battle here between Cormac Mac Art, and the Ulster men in 250 AD, in which the Ulster men were driven back as far as the Isle of Man.

In 1315 the Norman town of Granard was razed to the ground by Edward Bruce (who also destroyed the Norman abbey at Abbeylara nearby). Norman power was now in decline and the old medieval site of the town abandoned. Finally in 1586, English control was re-established. But Granard was still in the path of conflicting armies. During the Williamite Wars, it became a military base for King James' forces. 100 years later in 1798 when the French landed at Killala, a local force of United Irishmen rose in sympathy and tried to seize the town. They were defeated and 150 "rebels" were captured and hanged. Even in the 20th century, Granard was caught up in war. Michael Collins would come secretly to visit his fiancée here, Kitty Kiernan, whose family owned Granard's only hotel, the Greville Arms. In October, 1920, the Black and Tans roared into town and set fire to 14 houses. 4 months later, Sean McEoin, "the blacksmith from Ballinalee", successfully ambushed a Black and Tan unit just outside the town of Clonfin.

The main street at Granard with the Norman motte behind. Gallows on the hill, left, commemorate the hanging of United Irish" rebels" during the Rising of 1798. MARY SMYTH

Stone circle at Catrionbore – only a few stones remain. HECTOR MCDONNELL

Abbeylara (53.7652927,-7.4576209) The village name comes from the Cistercian Abbey founded by Richard de Tuite, the lord of Granard, with monks drawn from St Mary's Abbey in Dublin. But it was plundered and burnt by Edward Bruce, brother of Robert the Bruce in 1315 and not much survives today. On the south wall of the central crossing is a badly weathered sheela na gig. The last abbot was Richard O'Farrell who surrendered the abbey and its townlands to Henry VIII in 1540.

The Cartronbore Stone Circle (53.7829187,-7.4658619) 2km northeast of Granard. (Take the N55, then turn right onto R194, and look for the circle 2km along in a field on the right.) Stone circles were once built all over Europe, usually orientated to show the sun's setting or rising. This one has lost most of its stones. The stones are so-called glacial erratics deposited by a retreating glacier around 10,000 BC.

Edgeworthstown (53.6963317,-7.6826634) Once home to one of Ireland's most successful writers, Maria Edgeworth, who was famous for her novels (such as *Castle Rackrent* and *The Absentee*) and for her childrens' stories. The Edgeworths were enlightened landlords and did much to improve the town (*see page 24*). She and her father were also pioneers of s new system for teaching children (Practical Education) and later her brother ran a model school here. The family house (you can see the blocked up entrance at the east end of the main street) is now a nursing home, but there is a permanent exhibition about the Edgeworths in an old schoolhouse, the **Maria Edgeworth Centre**

Portrait of the Edgeworth family by Adam Buck, 1787.
Maria Edgeworth (with straw hat) is on the extreme left opposite her father.

(signposted off the main street) and an active Edgeworth Society who usually hold an annual literary festival here and can arrange guided tours of the town. WEBSITE: *edgeworthstown.net*

Edgeworthstown house in the 1790s with children playing outside.
WATERCOLOUR BY MARY POWYS, 1791

Early 17th century tomb of Sir Nathaniel Fox in Rathreagh chapel, Legan. By 1800, his effigy had already lost its head. HECTOR MCDONNELL

Rathreagh Church Just east of Legan on the border between Longford and Westmeath is this little gem of Jacobean architecture. The chapel was built in 1634 by Sir Nathaniel Fox, whose effigy (now headless) lies on the handsome tomb inside. Above him float winged angels and sphinxes, and below him, an inscription boasts of his son's marriage to Lord Dunsany's daughter.

The Foxes were descended from the Gaelic O'Sionnagh, (which translates as Fox), who once ruled the kingdom of Teffia in these parts. In the 16th century they worked with the English government and were granted lands taken from the O'Farrells. Sir Nathaniel also built a great house here, Foxhall, but almost nothing remains but a heap of stones and the farmyard buildings. Two of his descendants married daughters of the Edgeworth family from nearby Edgeworthstown, and Maria Edgeworth in her letters records many visits to Foxhall to admire the tomb of the already "headless knight".

Ardagh (53.6671618,-7.7028448) Now a model Victorian village set around a tiny triangular green. The gabled houses were designed by a noted Dublin architect, J. Rawston Carroll for Sir Thomas Fetherston in 1862, to commemorate his uncle, the previous landowner, and the uncle's widow added an elaborately pinnacled **Gothick clocktower** at a focal point. The inscription on it records her husband's "lifelong devotion to the moral and social improvement of his tenantry".

Ardagh House on the north side of the village green) is said to have been the inspiration for Oliver Goldsmith's play *She Stoops to Conquer* in which the hero mistakes the local squire's house for an inn. The play was based on a trick played on Goldsmith himself by a fellow student, who had once suggested to Goldsmith he should ask for lodgings here – much to Squire Fetherston's indignation. The house and its handsome stableyard is now sadly empty and falling into ruin.

St Patrick is said to have founded a church here in the 5th century, and consecrated his nephew, St Mel as the first bishop of Ardagh. All that remains is a small roofless chapel in the grounds of the parish church, made up of stupendous masonry with stones 2.5m long and 0.9m deep.

One of the stones was used as the foundation stone for the magnificent 19th century cathedral of **St Mel's** in the town of Longford.

Monument to an improving landlord, the clocktower at Ardagh erected in memory of Sir Thomas Fetherston, by his widow. 1862. PHOTO: THOMAS PAKENHAM

The Corlea Trackway (53.6125356,-7.8475274) Set in bogland at Keenagh, 8km north of Ballymahon, this extraordinary Iron Age trackway was excavated in the 1960s by Professor Raftery of UCD and was later given its own interpretive visitor centre. 18m of oak planks are on display, with 80m still buried under bog. The planks are wider than in any other Iron Age track discovered in Europe. It may have been designed as a ceremonial road for chariots but it is thought that the oak planks were so heavy they almost immediately sank into the bog.

Many earlier trackways have been discovered under bogs nearby, some dating from 4,000 BC, but most are made up of packed hazel, birch and alder placed lengthways to the track with only occasional cross timbers for support.

Saints Island (53.5524962,-7.9116255) on the northeastern shore of Lough Ree, can be reached via winding country roads and a narrow causeway 1km long. The Augustinian priory on the western shore was built in the 6th century by St Ciaran who later founded the monastery at Clonmacnoise. The

Ruins of the Augustinian priory on Saints Island, Lough Ree, early 1800s. It is still unchanged today. WATERCOLOUR BY DANIEL GROSE

Rathcline Castle on the shores of Lough Ree. Once "a noble and spacious house", it was destroyed during the Williamite Wars. WATERCOLOUR BY DANIEL GROSE, EARLY 1800S

abbey was plundered by the Danes in 1089; and was rebuilt in the early 13th century by the Dillons and survived precariously under their protection until the 17th century. Half buried cloisters now form little bridges in the grass but the church nave is still standing with a fine triple light window at one end.

Rathcline Castle (53.6512862,-8006681) 3.2km southeast of Lanesborough A large ruined castle on the shores of Lough Ree, it was originally owned by the Quinns, who built 2 adjoining tower houses here in the 15th century. In the 1660s it was bought by Sir George Lane, a faithful Royalist who had followed Charles II into exile. He was rewarded by being made Secretary of State for Ireland which post he held until his death in 1683. He seems to have remodelled the place with a long building linking the two tower houses and in 1682, it was described as "a very noble and spacious house...well improved with Orchards, Gardens, Fishponds and a Deer Park."

But all were ravaged soon after during the Williamite Wars and the castle

141

was abandoned. In the 1770s, Sir George Lane's descendants sold it to a rich Dublin businessman, Luke White who built Rathcline House nearby.

Not much remains now inside the walls. You can see a huge limestone fireplace on the first floor of the north wall, and there are two classical doorways, one to the south and one to the west.

Clondra (53.7320118,-7.906884). A picture postcard village straddling the river Camlin and the Royal Canal with a navigation channel cut through to the Shannon north of Lough Ree. The pretty harbour was purpose built in 1817 for the canal boats and housing for the harbour master and lockkeepers and an inn for travellers. But the Royal Canal never attracted as much traffic as had been hoped and was made redundant by the railway twenty years after it was completed. But it was re-opened for recreational traffic in 2010 and the restored harbour is now full of boats (mainly used to cruise the Shannon). There is a small hotel (the Richmond Inn) a couple of bars, and seating where you can drink or picnic in the sun. Cross the handsome stone bridge to admire the water wheel under the huge Victorian stone flour mill on the far side.

Richmond Harbour, Clondra, purpose built in the early 1800s to service the Royal Canal. Still a great place to moor a boat or picnic in the sun.